D1468281

Master Players

Learning from Children at Play

Gretchen Reynolds
Elizabeth Jones

Teachers College
Columbia University
New York and London

Published by Teachers College Press, 1234 Amsterdam Avenue, New York, NY 10027

Library of Congress Cataloging-in-Publication Data

Reynolds, Gretchen.
    Master players : learning from children at play / Gretchen
Reynolds, Elizabeth Jones.
        p.   cm.   — (Early childhood education)
    Includes bibliographical references (p.   ) and index.
    ISBN 0-8077-3582-5 (cloth : alk. paper). — ISBN 0-8077-3581-7
(paper : alk. paper)
    1. Play.   2. Early childhood education.   I. Jones, Elizabeth,
1930–   . II. Title.   III. Series: Early childhood education (New
York, N.Y.)
LB1137.R49   1997
155.418—dc20   96-41868

ISBN 0-8077-3581-7 (paper)
ISBN 0-8077-3582-5 (cloth)

Printed on acid-free paper

Manufactured in the United States of America

04   03   02   01   00   99   98   97   8   7   6   5   4   3   2   1

Contents

Foreword

Over the last decade children's play has received increasing attention not only from the early childhood profession but from organizations representing that profession, from researchers in child development, from practitioners, from those who design policies affecting children, from toymakers, and from the publication field. However, there is still a high incidence of disbelief among some early childhood practitioners and in society at large, that children's play provides both the most appropriate core and the most effective mechanism for a rich, pluralistic, and implementable early childhood curriculum. The fact that a highly respected professional organization, such as NAEYC, has developed a very well received position statement, *Developmentally appropriate practice for early childhood programs serving children from birth through age eight* (1987), does not seem to have provided a "wake-up call" sufficiently persuasive to allow this perspective to become more widely accepted.

It is becoming clear that a new paradigm must be devised to support researchers, teacher educators, practitioners, administrators, and policy makers as they learn to communicate their special perspectives to each other. I like to call this a "cross-pollinating" communications process. As it becomes widely utilized, it will allow the accrued knowledge of each specialty group with focus on children, child development, and/or children's play to begin to weave a new form of common practice. An increasingly holistic approach to the various aspects of child development, curriculum development, children's play, and family policy will begin to emerge and become more easily recognizable. Reynolds and Jones have provided a highly successful model for this effort through their writing and through their close and interconnected work with practitioners, administrators, and policy-makers.

The authors are also excellent models of strategic risk-taking. In ongoing ways, they share the findings of their research with their colleagues in the field and in such public arenas as professional conferences and the offering of their informal or in-process writings for critiquing by interested others.

Reynolds and Jones have taken courageous leadership as they focus upon moving the field forward. Each has a long-held interest and expertise in the field of children's play. I fully share that interest and have found it enriching to work with two such skilled professionals. They have been both presenters and active supporters of the Play, Policy and Practice Caucus, a newly formed, rapidly growing national body within the National Association for the Education of Young Children. In conjunction with the interdisciplinary membership of the caucus, Reynolds and Jones continue to work toward the development of a collective voice from the wide early childhood community, advocating the value and importance of children's play.

The authors of this volume continue to explicate the message that play is the most natural and effective way through which young children learn. Although many parents and teachers feel intuitively that play is important for children's growth and development, the tangible, but sometimes quite subtle, evidence of children's progress may be difficult to recognize. Meticulous observation, opportunities to reflect with others, and the reading of works such as this volume offer clarification and important opportunities to extend and deepen understanding.

It is fortunate that once again two of the field's keenest "watchers of children's play" have teamed up to make an important contribution. This volume builds upon the authors' earlier investigations, which appeared in their book, *The play's the thing: Teachers' roles in children's play* (1992). The current volume expands upon their view of how the power of careful observation and dialogue can result in respectful, insightful, and responsive practice. Through the presentation of richly developed case studies of four very diverse children, identified by their teachers as "master players," the authors demonstrate their powers of observation and their skills in utilizing a discussion format to make important points with clarity and impact. Reynolds served as the videographer. The two authors present their lively and thought-provoking discussion of each videographed observation as well as their sensitive and insightful analyses. In the process, the reader learns about the interface among child development; play theory; cognitive, social, emotional, and physical development; and ways to generalize findings to make them useful in work with other children.

In the process of reading this volume, the student of children and their play is introduced to a broad array of what a master teacher provides for children in the classroom. The idea that "real teaching" is occurring as long as the teacher is "in control" and exerting power over children is demonstrated to be a fallacy. The authors make a strong case for appropriately sharing power with children in reflective ways in order to support and enhance children's learning. They assert that there are now new roles and behaviors for the teacher to which we are not yet fully accustomed.

Through play facilitation, they contend, children can be helped to expand their curiosity and their competence, develop language with greater facility, and become more effective problem solvers. The authors outline some of the characteristics required for the role of the master teacher who supports children's play—a keen observer, an integrator of children's play, and one who can serve as both a scribe and a storyteller. This is no small task, they assure us, but it is such a rewarding and satisfying one!

Edgar Klugman
Wheelock College

Master Players

Learning from Children at Play

CHAPTER 1

The Concept of the "Master Player"

Dramatic and constructive play is one of the most valuable ways for young children to spend their time. Mastery of play is the developmental task at which 3-, 4-, and 5-year-olds are especially competent. A child plays spontaneously and with great satisfaction, often persisting despite a well-meaning adult's agenda for completion of a different task.

Play is the child's natural way of learning; it provides the time and opportunities children need to construct their own knowledge. Play poses an appropriate cognitive challenge as children use it in shaping social and physical worlds still unpredictable for them. Young children represent their experiences and feelings through play, entering into the long human tradition of symbol making in order to know. Play is a skill worth practicing and mastering—not, as adults often seem to think of it, a mere time filler or something to do outside to blow off steam. Mastering play is as important as mastering oral and written language. All these modes of symbolic representation enable human beings to remember, to manage, to plan, and to communicate with each other.

We use *master player* to describe the competence that we observe when a young child plays well. Parents and caregivers who get to spend time with young children know, enjoy, and are awed by the skills of master players. Like good theatre, "highly skilled" pretend play (Fein, 1987) amuses and entertains, because the audience sometimes see versions of themselves refreshingly mirrored in the behaviors of the actors.

At the end of a hectic day, Georgia, the teacher, takes time to relax and observe a small group of girls playing in the housekeeping corner. The resource teacher drops by to chat with her briefly. Wearing a floor-length green gown and high-heeled shoes, Sharon clomps toward them. She is pushing a doll carriage piled high with blankets and a brown grocery bag. Sharon pauses to smile at her two adult friends. Laughing, Georgia asks Sharon if she can show their visitor the contents of the bag.

1

Enjoying the adults' attention, Sharon grins and nods. Georgia first pulls out some plastic green beans, telling the resource teacher, "These are green beans." Then she takes out a plastic cauliflower and explains, quoting Sharon, "These are 'beets-with-no-color.'" As the adults giggle about Sharon's invented vegetable, she returns to her play.

The term *master player* has the potential to be misused. We don't think it should become a label that sets up comparisons among children, or be used as a standard against which to assess the skills of beginning players or to justify hothousing children in "play training" sessions. Rather, we find the concept useful because it communicates to others the value of children's quality play.

There are many ways to play, just as there are many languages. According to Wolf and Gardner (1979), children's approaches to play are a matter of individual play style; the playing child is either a "dramatist" or a "patterner." Dramatists prefer taking on roles, dramatic play, and games of strategy. Patterners are builders and artists, sensitive to the dimensions of objects such as color, size, and shape; they excel in visual and spatial tasks. However, in the skilled pretend play of the young child, these two activities are not as distinct as one might assume, or as has been suggested by research. In our opinion this is an artificial separation that may interfere with the observer's ability to value the totality of the play behaviors of which a master player is capable. Master players are both master dramatists and master artist/builders.

"Can we use the doctor stuff?" 5-year-old Rob asked his teacher. She agreed, and several children joined Rob in donning blue hospital gowns, stethoscopes, and surgical masks. They examined a blood pressure cuff, discussing the "doctor stuff" with each other.

"Let's get the blocks," said Rob to Tammy, and they pushed the cart of large blocks in from the hall. A platform was built in the rug area and spread out to extend over about one-fourth of the small classroom. Walls began to form. A doll was brought in and covered with a small afghan; La-Von and Amanda found the blood pressure cuff, which had been draped over the hospital wall, and began to care for the doll. At this point, eight children were playing in or around the block hospital. "I have to check your heart," said Rob to Amanda, putting a stethoscope to his ears.

When the structure appeared to be nearly completed, the teacher quietly brought out a collection of signs, laying them on a nearby table, at which she sat down. Some children were as enthusiastic about the signs as they had been about the doctor stuff and the blocks. One took a NO SMOKING sign and went for paper to make his own. Child-written signs began to appear all over the hospital. Meanwhile, three or four children ministered to the doll, and the now-empty block cart became an ambulance in which three children rode, another pushing. (Adapted from Daniels, 1988, pp. 79–82)

Children don't need to be "motivated" by a lesson plan in order to play. Play is what they do at every opportunity, what they do best and most attentively. Because play gives pleasure, it sustains itself, "having its aim in itself and accompanied by a feeling of tension, joy, and the consciousness that it is 'different' from 'ordinary life'" (Huizinga, 1950, p. 28). As any child will tell you, play is what you do because you want to. For adults and children alike, play is a self-chosen activity; in Csikszentmihalyi's (1975) word, it is *autotelic* behavior. Children's play is valuable for its own sake; it is the "child's right" (IPA and the Declaration of the Child's Right to Play, cited in Rivkin, 1995, p. 102).

PLAY AS REPRESENTATION

The play of 3-, 4-, and 5-year-olds, however, has a specific function. Master play is representational. It pictures and re-enacts the experiences children have had and can imagine having in the real world, within the safety of the small world of play that the child has created (Erikson, 1950). In play, young children are constructing their knowledge of the world by representing what they know. Play is children's self-chosen process of re-creating experience in order to understand it.

The beginnings of play seen in infants and toddlers are largely nonrepresentational; exploration of the physical world is the beginner's first priority. Preschoolers, as they continue to explore, elaborate their physical activity with complex representations of both real and imagined experiences. To represent is to communicate an abstract concept, an idea, or an experience by transforming it into a concrete form that can be seen, heard, touched, smelled, tasted, or combinations of these.

Representing what one knows, takes any and every form of self-expression available to humans: Picasso expressed himself in oils, Margaret Atwood writes poetry and novels, Nureyev chose ballet, ice sculptors celebrate winter in Ottawa, and young children have dramatic and constructive play. In "the hundred languages" at their disposal (Edwards, Gandini, & Forman, 1993), children re-create their world.

Mike and Tommy enjoy planning and making outfits for their dramatic play. Mike tells me, "Wait, silly, we have to get our costumes on, and then you can take a picture."

Tommy is talking to himself: "We can decorate something. You can make a mask for recognize. We could make a good mask, that could recognize."

Tommy links arms with Mike, and together they walk over to the art table. "Let's make some masks," Tommy says. "What do ya say? Alright? Now what do we have here?"

Each boy has a large sheet of red paper. Tommy takes a large bottle of white glue, and holding it upside down, begins making gluey lines on his paper. In a few moments he calls excitedly, "Hey, look at what I made, Mike! I made a Ninja Turtle!"

Mike comments, "Those are gonna be our disguises."

Tommy stands back to gaze at his paper, saying as he points, "There's our Ninja Turtle bellywear! Hey Mike, look at the Ninja! Mike, look at my Ninja Turtle I made! Mike!"

Mike, admiring Tommy's work, "Wow!"

Tommy stands back with his left hand on his hip, and asks, "Does it look like a Ninja Turtle? It looks like a Ninja Turtle to me! I'm gonna make some swords on it."

We are used to thinking of a representation as a product, a word-perfect or picture-perfect expression of significant experience. Masterful representations, however, are born out of a long sequence of acts as simple as telling a brief story, writing the first sentence on a piece of paper, or putting a doll in bed and waiting in the rocking chair beside her while she sleeps. Each of these bits of representation functions as learning, as a step in the learning process.

As many students (and writers) know, writing a paper can be like this. Sometimes it is very difficult to end a paper, to stop, to say (and feel) that it is finished. This happens because in the process of representing what one knows by writing, learning takes over. The first representations are a focus for corrections, additions, and the testing and expansion of ideas. Adult writers, artists, and actors are inclined to practice their craft in private. Young children are more generous in allowing us a window on the emergence of their ideas.

Lisa (age 3) was dictating a story to her teacher: "The wolf drived in his car and saw the three little pigs. Six pigs . . . "

Then she paused, looked up into the air and thought for a minute. At that point she seemed to be thinking of all the choices, editing in her mind before she spoke. She finished the story:

" . . . six pears, six popcorn, five bowls of dottie cereal. The three little pigs and a big horse that ate all their food. He had fur all over him. The black one." (Thornley, 1988, pp. 44–45)

Rather than learning to storytell or learning to write or learning to draw, practice of any of these skills is a continuous reciprocal process that Reggio Emilia educators regard as drawing to learn, where children "use their own field drawings for further work, such as making group murals, sculptures, paintings, and so forth" (Katz, 1993, p. 27). A teacher friend says it all; in his school-age program on the bulletin board, children's art is labeled "Masterpieces under Construction." Dyson (1989) has described the reciprocal process by which conversation, drawing, and writing all interweave among 5- to 8-year-old "friends learning to write." In early childhood, learning to storytell and storytelling to learn, which Lisa was practicing in the example above, take the form of "private speech," a phenomenon regarded by Vygotsky as "the centerpiece of development" (Berk & Winsler, 1995, p. 99).

Young children talk to themselves continually, especially when working on difficult tasks. Vygotsky argued that the child's self-talk is a "tool of thought — a means to direct his or her own attention and behavior. . . . The primary goal of private speech is not communication with others but communication with the self for the purpose of self-regulation, or guiding one's own thought processes and actions" (Berk & Winsler, 1995, p. 37). Private speech is basic to human consciousness, and adults do it as least as much as children do; they've just been socialized not to do it out loud. It's a form of play — experimentation and reflection without direct consequences in the real world.

Dewey, like Vygotsky, emphasized the reciprocal process by which understanding is constructed. According to Dewey (1916/1966),

> To "learn from experience" is to make a backward and forward connection between what we do to things and what we enjoy and suffer from things in consequence. Under such conditions, doing becomes a trying; an experiment with the world to find out what it is like; the undergoing becomes an instruction — the discovery of the connection of things. (p. 140)

In the parallel play of the very young, simultaneous private speech can be heard as children play and talk side by side, all intent on their own ideas. In the cooperative play of more skillful players, "the connection of things" is open for discovery not only through the backward and forward flow of the child's own actions, but in

> an ever-widening network . . . as children interact and create cause–effect situations for each other. Dramatic play becomes an arena in which each child brings his or her own world of personal meaning and, in encounter with others, has an opportunity to examine, amend, and order that world. (Cuffaro, 1995, p. 94)

Sociodramatic play requires children to negotiate their varied understandings so that play can go on. Play, being pretend, offers room for ingenious interweaving of fantasy and reality, feelings and facts. It can be built on whatever compromises the players are willing to accept; it need not be "true" from the perspective of the larger society.

In Cuffaro's words, in play "the child is . . . shuttling between self and world, and within self. As children 'experiment with the world to find out what it is like,' they make selections and connections and construct meaning" (p. 94), creating a representation of the world-they-can-live-in-right-now within the microcosm of their play.

PLAY, GAMES, AND EXPLORATION

In *play*, children invent the rules and patterns. Preschoolers are interested in games as well as in play, but in this stage, mastery of play should have priority.

Karla, age 4, is playing Concentration on the computer with her mother. The computer program enforces the rules of the game, and Karla needs lots of adult help to do it right. Later in the evening, however, her visiting grandmother suggests to Karla that they reinvent Concentration on the floor in her bedroom, laying out pairs of small stuffed animals and covering them with T-shirts from her dresser drawer. In this improvised game Karla is free to *play*, and she does with a vengeance; the rules of Concentration are redefined on the spot to ensure that on Karla's turns, she wins, and on her grandma's turns, grandma loses.

The playing child is in charge; in the small imaginary worlds of play, children, not adults, have the power. In *games*, in contrast, the rules and patterns have been invented by adults, and the challenge to the child is to master them. A puzzle is a game, in this sense; the child may choose the puzzle to "play with," but the task is to do the puzzle right. Soccer as played by adults and older children is a game with rules, and skills to be mastered within the framework of the rules. Soccer as played by younger children without adults in charge is play—a continual reinvention of the rules. Mastery of games, including most school tasks, is the primary developmental challenge for children beyond preschool and kindergarten.

Exploration is the beginning stage of approaching any new challenge. In earliest childhood, physical challenges dominate the child's experience; she must learn to sit, to crawl, to walk. Much of the activity of preschool children continues as exploration and practice: What happens when I paint over the red with this blue? Can I make it to the top of the climber? How fast will this tricycle go? Exploration play is invented by the child within the external rules that are decided and enforced by adults, either for safety reasons ("no throwing sand") or for reasons of community living ("we need to clean off the tables for lunch").

In exploration, younger children are using their bodies and are experimenting with things to see how they feel and what they do. The child is trying to find out, "What does this thing do?" (Hutt, 1982). Curiosity about the object motivates the child's actions.

Sometimes as an accompaniment to her movement, the beginning player tries out pretend play with objects—as she fiddles with the rotator dial on the plastic telephone, she asks into the receiver, "Hello?" Here she is moving from the exploration question, "What does this thing do?" to the play question, "What can I do with this thing?"

Mastery of physical skills and language is a precursor of master play, and sociodramatic play requires considerable social skills as well. The beginning players in an early childhood program are likely to be still at the stage of exploration and practice in these skills. Before one can experiment with the invention of complicated patterns, one has to have the basics down. Here's a 3-year-old practicing some basics.

Rolando is standing on the outdoor platform in preschool. At one side of the platform, dolls are being industriously bathed to the accompanying chatter of their 4-year-old "parents." At the other side, several taller children are running in an elaborate chase pattern—over the railing, down to the ground, up on top of the big box, then down and into the box, where they can hide from the bad guys; they're planning, loudly, as they run.

Rolando moves from one corner of the platform to the other, introducing a hop into his walk before he arrives at the other corner. He pauses, turns, hops twice, then retraces his steps at a run. He repeats the whole pattern and follows it with several new moves.

The big boys' chase pattern, which includes many of the same movements Rolando is working on privately, reflects their skill in coordinating movement, language, and dramatic script while simultaneously negotiating social roles. Rolando can't yet do all those things at once; next year or the year after, he will. He may even get a chance to try, this morning, if Keisha notices his movement pattern and decides to try it too, dangling a dripping doll by its arm. What will happen? Perhaps a dramatic play script ("The baby's going to sleep here while we go out"), perhaps a playful game-with-rules ("First you hop, then I hop"), or perhaps a confrontation ("Teacher, she's botherin' me!").

When children have had sufficient time to explore and become familiar with the things in the environment, the style and character of their play becomes quite different. The motivation for play is the child's own good ideas, and objects are used in nonliteral ways to express the child's meaning. While the child's behavior in exploration play reflects the function of the prop or toy, the master player uses toys and props and language imaginatively to symbolize ideas (El'konin, 1966; Hutt, 1982).

Kim is pushing dolls in two strollers; now she parks the strollers next to a large block structure, built earlier in the morning by other children, and sits down on it. Anna sits in front of her, conjures a steering wheel out of the air, and starts driving. Teresa arrives with her doll.
"You two are daughters, OK?" says Anna.
An argument follows. They're mommies, not daughters.
Anna gives in. "I go get my baby." She gets another doll from the house area and lays it on the vehicle; then she drives some more, making an up-and-down motion rather than her earlier circular steering-wheel motion. She stops driving and says, "Two babies."
"Drive, drive, drive!" yells the girl behind her, punching her.
"I'm the mommy," says Anna.
"Two mommies," says Kim, holding up two fingers.
"I driving, I driving," says Teresa, establishing herself as driver. Anna leaves briefly, then returns to put her baby in the stroller, adds a telephone to the structure, and starts driving again, with vigorous arm movements and singing.

Master players will initiate pretend play through a simple statement about an object or a role that signifies "this is pretend" to others—"You two are daughters, okay?" or "That will be our 'frigerator, right?" In naming the play, these communications establish an invisible boundary that frames and separates nonreal worlds from reality. "This is pretend" is the rule that identifies a context and structures the play (Bateson, 1955; Giffin, 1984). Master players willingly adapt their behaviors, interactions, ideas, and negotiations to the rules imposed by the play frame because rules challenge the skills of the players and sustain the play. Pretend play is unpredictable, because the rules are changed or modified, or new ones invented, continually. Rule changes occur seamlessly within the frame of the play, requiring unrehearsed, spontaneous responses of the players.

Several boxes have been set out in a group in the yard. These large wooden boxes were built by parents—they are open on one side, and they are large enough for several children. These are the "secluded places" (Fein, 1987) master players often require in the creation of private play worlds. The children, engrossed in the play, ignore the observer's intrusive video camera.

Jill, Robert, and Valerie are collaborating to evolve the plot and solve conflicts that arise as they play. Although the three have decided on a theme for their play, they are far from agreement about the roles each will take.

VALERIE: That will be our 'frigerator, right? Get the blankets!

JILL: Father, what are you doing?

ROBERT: I'm getting back here.

JILL (*Moving around outside the house on her hands and feet*): Say, "Get back in your bed."

ROBERT: Get back in your bed!

JILL (*dutifully crawling back into the box*): Go to sleep, Father, it's night!

VALERIE (*taking off her shoes*): Okay, Little Foot, here I come!

JILL (*Wrapped in a pink blanket, she closes her eyes for a split second.*): Morning!

VALERIE: Morning!

JILL: Who wants to be the grandma? I want Valerie to be the grandma!

VALERIE: I don't want to play the grandmother.

JILL: Well, Robert wants to play the mother really bad, right?

ROBERT: Right! We could have two moms.

JILL: I'm Little Foot, I'm the baby.

ROBERT: I know! We could have a girl Little Foot and a boy Little Foot.

JILL: I'm gonna be the girl Little Foot and he's gonna be the boy Little Foot.

VALERIE: And I'm the mom. And you two live in the same little room and I live next door. I live right there (*pointing to the next box*). I'm gonna get a mat and put it up there.

JILL: Can I sleep with you?

VALERIE: Yeah.

ROBERT: Can I sleep with you?

VALERIE: No, you have to sleep down there.

JILL (*She climbs up on top of the box next to Valerie.*): There's enough room up here for all of us, see?

VALERIE: Well, I'm sleeping in the middle then.

Children play to understand rules. The play worlds they create are as unpredictable as life. Because it challenges them, dramatic play is children's most competent behavior. In play, the child always behaves beyond his average age, above his daily behavior; in play it is as though he were a head taller than himself. As in the focus of a magnifying glass, play contains all developmental tendencies in a condensed form and is itself a major source of development. . . . Action in the imaginative sphere, in an imaginary situation, the creation of voluntary intentions, and the formation of real-life plans and volitional motives—all appear in play and make it the highest level of preschool development. (Vygotsky, 1933/1978, p. 102)

SUPPORTING CHILDREN'S MASTERY OF PLAY

The developmental task of the playing young child as "master dramatist" (Creaser, 1987, p. 30) is the healthy achievement of initiative through play (Erikson, 1950). Play is the arena in which young children appropriately can practice asserting themselves and taking initiative, particularly because it is the context in the child's life where adults have the least control. However, this does not imply that adult responsiveness to the child's play should be less than it would be to other kinds of behaviors. Rather, Erikson argued that significant people in the child's environment are important in affirming his or her initiative taking to support healthy identity development.

In this child care program the yard is shared by several groups. The 3-year-olds usually have a 15-minute wait after snack before they go outside. In the transition between eating and dressing to go out, one of the teachers cleans up the food and tables, while two other teachers watch over the children for a few minutes of free play. Pam, a student in her first year of early childhood education at the college, is sitting in a child-sized chair to one side of the play area where she can see all the children. Two boys are stacking cardboard blocks, and a third is guiding a truck around the floor. Four-year-old Maria approaches Pam. Putting a bowl at her feet, Maria squats down on her hands and knees and says, "Meow, meow, kitty wants some milk." Pam pays no attention. Maria tries again, "Meow, mommy, give kitty some milk!" When Pam does not respond this time, Maria wanders off.

An important teaching skill is *response-ability*, the ability of the adult to notice and respond to the initiative the child shows in play. When we discussed our perceptions with Pam, she said that at the time she was watching the whole group to make sure all the children were playing safely. Safety, of course, is the teacher's first concern, but it should not be her only concern. As Pam gains more experience, we hope she will expand her teaching skills to include the role of teacher as player (Jones & Reynolds,

1992). How often, we wonder, do adults overlook the initiative the child is taking when the medium is dramatic play? And for what reasons?

Modern day care poses many challenges to children and teachers alike. Child care regulations usually focus on safety and the child's well-being first. Teachers learn to master the clock (they have little choice to do otherwise), so that schedules can be maintained with predictable regularity day after day. Children may arrive between 7:30 and 8:00, breakfast between 8:30 and 8:50, play outside at 10:30, nap at 12:30, and so on.

> Rather than providing situations where children could engage in child-initiated activity, play freely with friends, and try out absorbing activities in an atmosphere of exploration and a climate of social responsibility, . . . day care centers more frequently operated like miniature factories, with fixed time periods for activities and children moving through them as if they were in an assembly line: 9:30 was snack time, no matter how absorbed Susan and Graham might have become in making fingerprint designs. (Wien, 1995, p. 2)

So that the day can proceed safely, efficiently, and pleasantly enough, children's behavior during transitions and routines is molded; they learn to sit quietly on the bus, tidy up their own and others' messes, and eat first, talk later. The routines and transitions are a solution to the challenge of how adults and children can live together reasonably as a child care community. Most teachers will admit that the times when children are asked to accommodate to schedules and routines, and to teachers' agendas, are not the times of the day when children thrive. Children are at their best when creating their own reality.

Vivian Paley (1986), reflecting on her observations of young children in her classroom, comments:

> "Let's pretend" was a stronger glue than any preplanned list of topics, and the need to make friends, assuage jealousy, and gain a sense of one's own destiny provided better reasons for self-control than all my disciplinary devices. A different reality coexisted beside my own, containing more vitality, originality, and wide-open potential than could be found in any lesson plan. (p. 124)

The young master player is competent because she is playing. Time for play is valuable because play is the child's most comfortable medium—in play the child is sharp. Because 4- and 5-year-olds are at their best when they are playing, it is the mode that allows them to practice other skills: taking initiative and solving problems within the constraints of a task or rules, focusing attention for long periods of time, negotiating social relationships, inventing and imposing patterns and order, and manipulating materials and ideas in creative ways. These are skills that cannot be taught directly, but they are learned by children in play. Young children know how to grow: They play to get better at it and they play to learn.

What, then, is left for their teacher to do?

CHAPTER 2

Play Watching

Our book *The Play's the Thing* (Jones & Reynolds, 1992) is all about teachers' roles in children's play. Our basic premise is that "the skillful teacher of young children is one who makes . . . play possible and helps children keep getting better at it" (p. 1). To do this, the teacher stage-manages, mediates, and may play with beginning players, until their mastery of play frees her to focus her energies on the subject of this chapter, play watching.

Many teachers, parents, and supervisors, however, think of "teaching" as teacher action directed toward children—leading a group, reading a story, giving verbal directions or information. "I'll come back when you're teaching," one supervisor on an evaluation visit was heard to say to a teacher who was busy observing children at play. Some teachers feel shut out of children's play because they have not taught the children how to do it; frequently, such teachers interrupt children's play with ideas of their own that get them back in charge of the action.

In developmental fact, however, the quality of the play in a classroom for 3- to 5-year-olds is the measure of a teacher's success. Skilled pretend play mirrors cognitive and social competence. The concept of *master player* encourages teachers to reflect on the conditions and interventions that sustain children's participation in complex play. It becomes a framework against which one's teaching practices are accountable.

The teacher, then, is challenged to become a skilled play watcher. The appropriate method for assessing young children's skills is observation, a heuristic mode of inquiry through which the teacher can learn about the child's needs and the effectiveness of her own interventions. Observation can be used not only as the basis of information about individual children and the building of a classroom community, but also as the place from which teachers can begin to engage in the dialogic process of reflection, hypothesis building, and planning. This book is about play watching. It takes the form of dialogue between the authors, both devoted play watchers.

OBSERVING CHILDREN AT PLAY

Play watching takes many forms. In our own teaching and observing we have at various times written anecdotal notes, running records, time samples, and checklists; taken photos and videotapes; saved samples of children's work and made sketches to capture block buildings and dramatic play episodes; exclaimed to a colleague, "Did you see *that*?" and talked about what we saw; and, sometimes, simply enjoyed the play without making any record at all. All this practice has made us increasingly aware of the details of children's behavior, so that our sensitivity to nuances makes us effortlessly competent observers. We can now kid watch for the sheer joy of it, seeing and recording a great deal without having to pay attention to the techniques of doing so.

The most difficult observation challenge either of us has experienced was learning the coding of the Child's Mode of Behavior in the Child Behavior Inventory (Prescott, Jones, Kritchevsky, Milich, & Haselhoef, 1975), which has been the inspiration for this book. Betty helped in the development of the inventory in the 1970s, as part of a study of quality in child care. Gretchen made use of it in the 1990s in her research on master players, having previously learned it in a class with Liz Prescott at Pacific Oaks College. In the child care project, the research team coded child behavior on site, as it was happening, tallying behaviors on a grid every 15 seconds. If the observers didn't get them, they were gone. In the master players study, two researchers coded videotapes of child behavior, which made replays possible at moments of confusion.

Why, if it's all that hard to learn, are we writing a book about it? Because it's such fun to play with. Once mastered, it's a whole new language to be spoken with other initiates: "That kid's T3ing, right?" "I'm not so sure. It looks to me as if she's settled into I2." Like any new language, it creates a novel and stimulating world view.

Mostly, in this book, we'll be speaking standard English rather than "behavioral code"; the reader will be able to sail through the stories of children in Chapters 3 to 6 encountering only a handful of T, I, or E codes. In the last few chapters, however, we will be indulging ourselves by referring to the coding categories in our dialogue about what we've seen in the case studies—first to analyze the components of children's master play, and then in Chapter 10 to experiment with applying the codes to the behavior of teachers supporting children's play.

For readers ready to be told what on earth this is all about, in the next section we present an overview of the Child's Mode of Behavior coding. Other readers—those who want to get on to the case studies of the children—are invited to skip to Chapter 3, returning later to read about the code if they get curious. The Appendix contains Elizabeth Prescott's description of how she has used the code in teaching college classes on observing and recording child behavior.

CODING CHILD BEHAVIOR

The Child's Mode of Behavior coding (Prescott et al., 1975) reflects four categories of human behavior, identified in the code by capital letters: *rejects* (R), *thrusts* (T), *responds* (E), and *integrates* (I). Within each category there are four to seven variations, which are numbered.

Rejecting behavior is defined as "refuses input, either actively or passively, by ignoring, avoiding, rejecting, or negating. He either refuses to let something into his world, or behaves so as to eliminate something that is there" (p. 3). The rejecting child may ignore, avoid, or actively seek to eliminate intrusion. Using examples adapted from the Child Behavior Inventory (Prescott et al., 1975), the following list shows how the code combines the category letters with the numbered variations.

R1 Ignores
  • Three children rush noisily up to the carpentry table close to John. John takes no notice, continues hammering.
  • Teacher says, "Time for juice." John continues hammering.
R2 Avoids
  • Several children rush noisily up to the carpentry table. John, who has been hammering, moves away to the nearby fence.
R3 Active
  • Child reaches for John's cupcake. John says, "Stop that!"
R4 Aggressive
  • Child reaches for John's cupcake. John says, "Stop that!" and punches the child.
  • Teacher says, "John, sit down." John says, "No," and kicks the teacher.

Thrusting behavior involves "thrusting outward, initiative; provides new or additional input by actively intruding, seeking, selecting, initiating, or offering" (p. 4). The thrusting child independently starts something. Examples of four of the seven categories of thrusting follow:

T2 Gives orders
  • Child tells others, "Stay away from the rabbit."
T3 Chooses activity

- Child gets the truck off the shelf.
- Child walks up to someone and says "hello."

T5 Asks for help
- Child asks, "Where are the nails?"
- Crying child comes to the teacher.

T6 Gives information, opinion
- Child announces, "My cat had kittens."
- Child exclaims, "You're a dumbbell!"

Responding behavior "takes account of immediate or just previous input, either passively by receiving, or actively by matching response to input" (p. 6). The responding child is attending to cues in the physical or social environment, as shown in these examples.

E1 Perceptually receptive
- Child watches as other children converse.

E2 Obeys, cooperates, imitates
- Child picks up toys on request.
- Child rolls a clay snake, copying another child.

E5 Receives positive input
- Child receives more paste from the teacher.

E6 Responds to questions
- In response, the child tells the teacher where the paint is.

The most complex form of behavior in this scheme is *integrative behavior*, in which "action shows both initiation and response to context. Response is individual, but fits into the continuity of action" (p. 7). Integrative behavior is particularly characteristic of play, as Smilansky (1968) has noted. It is coded in six variations, with further divisions within a variation indicated by a lowercase letter. The complete "integrates" category follows:

I1 Problem solving

I1a Shows recognition of built-in constraints; problem solves. Elaborates in a closed situation. Behavior involves both response and initiation, implying skill in a task that has right and wrong aspects.
- Child fits piece into the puzzle.
- Child says, "That's the letter C."

I1b Copes effectively with social constraints. Child spontaneously shows understanding of the social system and/or effectively asserts own desires within the social system.

• Teacher says, "I want everyone to wash up now." Child says, "I just washed up when I went to the bathroom. Can I read a little longer?"

I2   Attends with concentration to the activity.

• Child adds blocks to tower that he and another child are building.

I3   Adds something new: a suggestion, a play idea, a physical prop.

• Child adds water to a sand pile.

• Child says, "Hey, we could build a skyscraper."

I4   Shows mutuality in social interaction.

I4a Reciprocity

• Children invent a song as they swing.

I4b Offers sympathy, help, affection

• Child comforts another child who is crying.

I4c Hostile reciprocity

• Two children swing together, calling insults to each other.

• Children make up a game by punching each other.

I5   Sees patterns or gives structure; responds in an ambiguous situation with novel but fitting constraints; imposes self-generated figure–ground relationships on ambiguous setting.

• Child says, "Look, if I turn it this way, it could be a roof."

I6   Tests, tinkers, examines; shows real curiosity and attentiveness.

• Child carefully examines a toy truck, checking out each moving part.

Integrative behavior is intentional and complex; it is responsive to things as they are but often transforms them into new creations initiated by the child. It demonstrates the master player's ability to come to terms with the real world while envisioning a world that might be—a skill of supreme value in human living.

USING THE CODE

As noted earlier, I (Gretchen) used the Child's Mode of Behavior code in my research on master players (Reynolds, 1992). I observed children's play for 2½ months in five early childhood education programs in Pasadena, California. Two were private programs at the Children's School at Pacific Oaks College: La Loma Preschool program and Burgess House Child Care. The three other programs were public preschools funded by the State of California and sponsored by the Pasadena Unified School District (PUSD).

The Children's School programs and the PUSD preschools were philo-
sophically similar: They valued the young child's learning through self-
selected activities, interactions with peers and significant adults, and play.
The teachers in all of the programs scheduled a balance of teacher-led,
small-group activities with longer periods of free play. The PUSD preschools
were modeled on the High/Scope curriculum, in which free play (work
time) lasted at least 45 minutes. At La Loma Preschool and Burgess House,
free play was 1½ to 2 hours.

In all the programs the environments supported the children's free movement among a variety of learning areas, including an art center, a house
play area, a block-building area, and table manipulatives. Games and loose
parts were stored on open shelves, where they were both accessible and
supportive of children's participation in cleanup. Activities that varied from
day to day were sand play, water play, woodworking, clay work, and play
dough. Teachers supported children's play in specific areas by providing
props and facilitating conflict resolution. The children at Burgess House
and La Loma Preschool played both indoors and outside in the yard during
free play. To maintain appropriate ratios, teachers were flexible in moving
around the environment as children's involvement shifted.

The five programs served, in combination, an ethnically and economi-
cally diverse population. The research sample of 40 children included 18
African-Americans, 10 Euro-Americans, seven Mexican-Americans, three
Japanese-Americans, one Chinese-American child, and one Japanese-
Mexican child. Spanish was spoken in the homes of six of the children; all
the other families spoke English. Twenty-four of the children were from
families with low or poverty-level incomes. The families of 16 children were
middle/upper-middle-income earners.

Half of the 40 children were identified by their teachers as "master
players," and half as "unskilled players." There were 21 girls and 19 boys.
The average age of the master players was 50 months, of the unskilled
players, 43 months. I videotaped one child at a time during free play, for 5
to 10 minutes at a time. When the target child was engaged in play with
other children, I maintained the focus of the camera on that child, while
seeking to capture as many of the actions of his or her co-players as possible.

A total of 226 samples of children's play were collected on tape in this
way. Because of the children's irregular attendance, the number of filmings
for each of the children varied from three to seven, with an average of five
to six. The videotapes were later analyzed using the Child's Mode of Behavior coding, with the objective of exposing patterns of behavior characteristic of master players.

I anticipated that differences between preschool master players and unskilled players, as nominated by their teachers, would surface in the *integrates* category as the observations of the children's play were coded. In fact, four integrative behaviors were manifested significantly more often by master players.

I1b Copes effectively with social constraints
I3   Adds something new
I4   Shows mutuality in social interaction
I5   Sees patterns or gives structure

I found that I left each filming session stimulated, full of thoughts and questions about the events that had occurred. I made notes at the computer as I viewed each day's videotape. Through this writing I began the process of reflection and hypothesis building about the children, their play, and the effects of the environment on their play. I wrote down stories of my interactions with the teachers; thoughts about schedules, the use of space, materials, and equipment; insights about specific children; and things to look for the next time I was to film.

Wassermann (1993) calls this kind of a process "meaning making."

> Making meaning of the events in the classroom is what we teachers do, from moment to moment, every teaching day. We "size up" a situation, reflect on what it means, and choose an appropriate action that depends upon how we have interpreted the event. This is how we teach ourselves to understand "what is happening" . . . to determine the action to take. (p. 11)

LEARNING THROUGH DIALOGUE

We teach ourselves most fruitfully in dialogue with others. In this research the opportunity for dialogue was built in at two points.

Because I expected that the teachers would be a valuable source of information regarding the children's play lives at school, I scheduled an interview with each head teacher at the end of the data-gathering process. The teachers brought warmth, openness, and sincerity to the interviews; they were eager to share their perceptions of the children. I found that a second perspective on the children greatly enriched my own understanding of them. I had not, however, anticipated the extent to which the interview process would expose new insights about the teachers, their programs, and their personal teaching philosophies.

In reflecting on the interview process, I realized that my relationship with all the teachers had grown. I wondered if the interviews served, as well, as a form of self-expression for the teachers, enabling them to receive the recognition of a peer who held similar values in an "association of kindred minds" (Erikson, 1980, p. 120). Our dialogue may have given the teachers an opportunity to mirror their natural talents, to experience "self-recognition coupled with a mutual recognition" (p. 122).

A second opportunity for dialogue involved learning to use the code while simultaneously training a research assistant. The task was to assign a code to the child's videotaped behavior every 15 seconds. In the effort to do this with accuracy and consistency, the research assistant and I practiced together for several days. The first sessions were especially difficult; one day we spent 2 hours attempting to reach agreement on the coding for 7 minutes of tape.

Elizabeth Prescott, who had developed the codes, was consulted by telephone; Betty, who had participated in Prescott's 1975 study, joined us in discussion of what we were seeing on the tape. Her familiarity with the codes and her insights into the meaning of the children's play behaviors helped in clarifying definitions. She also helped us appreciate the value of disagreement and discussion as a way of arriving at mutual clarity.

The meetings with the children's teachers and the subsequent coding work with Betty and the research assistant taught me how much fuller the insights into children's play are when several people exchange perspectives. Over a cup of frozen yogurt, Betty and I agreed that a book might be a way of "going public" about the value of dialogue in understanding children's play.

The four chapters that follow present case examples based on transcripts made from my videotapes. Each highlights a selected master player and his or her mode of patterning his or her experience of the world. (The names used are pseudonyms.) The cases are presented in the context of our dialogue about them: the next stage of the dialogue process just described. Beginning with a selected transcript, each of us wrote our interpretive comments on it, then traded them and wrote some more. We were proceeding on the assumption that dialogue — oral and written — among play watchers is a significant process of increasing individual and mutual understanding of what we are seeing; and that our modeling of the process as we experienced it, may serve to enlighten and challenge others to try it for themselves.

CHAPTER 3

Tommy: Seeking Power in Play

TRAPPERS

Tommy is in the yard. He is working to pull a rope across the walkway so that he can tie it to the posts on either side. All around him is the noisy activity of children hard at play, none of it interfering with Tommy's concentration. As he works Tommy talks to himself and chants "boom boom boom, boom boom boom," and "I'm gonna pull on this. . . . " One can hear Mike's voice echoing Tommy's as he plays nearby with a rope of his own: "Boom boom boom baba boom boom boom."

Tommy realizes that the rope is not long enough. He pulls it apart to unravel the braid, and now he has two single strands, which when knotted are long enough to stretch between the two pipes. He continues chanting "switch . . . ditch . . . ditch."

Tommy knots the rope on one post by weaving the end through a lump of rope. He crosses the walk and pulls the rope taut. He weaves the other end of the rope around the opposite pipe. Tommy stands back to survey his work. "Now people will go boom boom boom. Mike! Mike, you want to know something? Now people will go 'boom boom boom' when they're running. People will go trip right over the rope when they're running. They go 'boom boom boom,' and they'll fall down!"

Dave, a caregiver, has been keeping an eye on the children's rope play. Tommy turns to him, "Dave, try to run. . . . "

DAVE: Try to walk across there?

TOMMY (*laughing*): Yeah.

DAVE (*He pretends he is a person on the path unaware of the "rope trap." He walks toward the rope and feigns tripping over it.*): What happens? Whoop!

TOMMY (*laughing at him*): A-ha trick I did!

DAVE: You're a pretty tricky guy, I must say.

TOMMY (*pointing*): Trick on one side of the street and on the other side.

DAVE: Pretty tricky stuff.

Betty: How fortunate Tommy is to have such a playful teacher! Trappers need someone to fall into their traps. And Dave plays beautifully, appreciating Tommy as a pretty tricky guy.

Gretchen: Dave is a great match for Tommy, and Tommy thoroughly enjoys him. Unlike some other adults, Dave remembers that children know that play isn't real. Tommy, he knows, is pretending, and so is he.

Betty: For many adults this wouldn't be acceptable play, would it? They'd take it seriously and be horrified by the idea of a child's trying to trip people with a rope. Where did the ropes come from?

Gretchen: Dave found them a few days earlier in a friend's garage and brought them in to day care. Several of the children were very excited about having real ropes to play with—Tommy and Mike especially.

Betty: I'd think so! Tommy was having a wonderful idea (Duckworth, 1996), and it was clearly play, not reality, as you said. The rope was visible to everyone, but this was play so it was invisible. The innocent victim pretended to trip; he didn't really trip.

Gretchen: And Dave, of course, wasn't Tommy's enemy; he's Tommy's play buddy. Tommy could count on him to play by Tommy's rules. Dave's dependable that way; he's ready to respond to and encourage children's initiative. I think of it as "response-ability."

Betty: I like that. He's one of those master teachers of 4-year-olds who really trust that children learn through play. They can remain near playing children, watching and waiting; Janet Gonzalez-Mena describes it as "wanting nothing," but being sensitively aware of when they might be useful to the child (Gonzalez-Mena & Eyer, 1989).

Gretchen: This is Tommy's second year at Burgess House, the day care program at the Pacific Oaks Children's School. Tommy is a 4-year-old Euro-American child with a tuft of reddish-brown hair and is very competent physically and verbally. His favorite phrase at the moment is "Hello, babe!" Tommy and Mike usually concur in the afternoons about the clothes they will wear to day care the next day, so they are suitably dressed for whatever play they are planning. One day recently they wore firefighter outfits, playing up the swaggering, macho image that can be a stereotype of male firefighters.

Then there was the day when Tommy had a real enemy—me with my video camera.

Betty: Did the children know you would be filming or did you just show up in the yard one day? I suppose that from a playing child's point of view, an observer who quietly sits on the floor or on a low stool and takes notes is a lot less intrusive than someone with a video camera on her shoulder. People of all ages are self-conscious around cameras.

Gretchen: The children's responses to the video camera were so varied!

I remembered to get permission from all the parents before I began filming, but it wasn't until we analyzed the videotapes that I realized I had been pretty cavalier in not talking with the children about who I was and why I wanted to film their play.

Betty: You were a bit of an unknown element, weren't you? Since you hadn't informed the children, we've seen on the videotapes lots of different responses by children as they attempted to figure you out—to find ways to get control or exert their power over a possibly dangerous adult.

Gretchen: In hindsight, it would have been friendly to invite the children to ask me questions about the video camera—high tech things fascinate kids.

When I arrived for the next observation Tommy and Mike were busy in the sandbox. Tommy was trying to tie a small rope onto the handle of an eggbeater. Mike spotted me and warned, "We not letting you take a picture of us!"

ZAPPERS

Wary because of Mike's greeting, I asked: "Should I come back a little later, Tommy, or can I film you now?"

TOMMY: No. Nothing.

GRETCHEN: What? I'm sorry, I didn't hear you.

TOMMY: I hate you.

GRETCHEN: You hate my filming you?

TOMMY: Yeah.

GRETCHEN: Why?

TOMMY: 'Cause I want to slice off your head.

GRETCHEN (*laughing, because I don't know how to get out of this grace-
    fully*): Well, I'll grow another one then!

TOMMY (*smiling, to Mike*): Mike, can you please . . . this dirty woman . . .
    chop off her head!

GRETCHEN: Do you know my name? Maybe I never told you. It's Gretchen.

MIKE: Now I know your name, Gretchen! I hate that name.

TOMMY (*He has finished tying the rope onto the eggbeater. He hoists it back
    over his shoulder.*): I hate this. Catch that! (*He playfully casts the egg-
    beater trap in my direction. Then, to Mike*): Mike, connect this on to
    something. I'll show you where to connect it on to.

Mike is watching. Tommy takes the end of the rope over to the post. As he is wrapping it around the post, he gives directions to Mike: "You push this button and then I'll . . . " Skillfully Tommy ties the end of the rope in a knot. He calls, "Ready? Mike, Mike here's the zapper! Try a but-

ton . . . I'm gonna zap her! You want me to zap her? I'll zap her if you want
me to!"

Mike goes over to the post. Pretending, he presses the "button."
Tommy turns the squeaky handle of the eggbeater, aiming it at me. "This
is a dead zapper." He briefly examines the web that has been created by
the wrapping of the rope around the post, and hangs up his eggbeater
weapon as in a cradle. Then he picks it up again, aims it at me, and makes
shooting noises.

GRETCHEN: Oh, that one went right over my head. I heard it go past. You
    know what, you missed, and it got Mike by mistake.

TOMMY (*grinning*): Uh-uh. (*He shoots at me again.*)

MIKE: Get her in the eye, Tommy.

GRETCHEN: It deflected off me and hit Mike!

MIKE (*falling over "dead"*): John is making poison to pour on you.

GRETCHEN: I'm invincible to poison.

MIKE: No, you're not. I'll pour it on you for real.

JOHN: I'm going to pour bubble poison on you, and the soap will get on
    you and you'll die.

A caregiver has been listening to this exchange: "You know what, how I
    don't let you hit other kids? Well, I don't let you hurt adults and their
    stuff either."

TOMMY (*making shooting noises and turning the zapper in the direction of
    the porch*): This is a paint blatter that blows people's eyes out. (*He re-
    turns to the sandbox with an ice cream scoop.*) I'll put something on
    this, it's a special kind of dirt. Special kind of dirt. (*He scoops sand
    onto the end of the beater, banging it with a scoop.*) This is a special
    kind of paint blatter. Special kind of paint blatter. Has paint in it. (*He
    stands and aims the blatter at the porch.*) You squirt it at your hair, your
    eyes, and your mouth. Electric paint blatter!

CAREGIVER: Tommy, I don't like you to aim that at me. (*Tommy stops.
    Mike hangs up the paint blatter zapper.*)

Several minutes later Tommy brings over a strip of stickers from the
art table. A sticker is on Tommy's cheek. Tommy holds the strip out for
Mike, who puts a sticker on the back of his hand. John says to Mike, "We
have to put on our costumes so the teachers don't know who we are."
John says to me, "Wait, silly, we have to get our costumes on, then you
can take a picture."

Mike goes over to Tommy to get another sticker.

TOMMY: We have to get our special costumes.

MIKE (*turning to a child*): Want a sticker? You get them wet and they stick
    on. (*He licks a sticker and puts it on the front of the child's shirt.*) Put it
    on you.

TOMMY: Put it on your eye so the teachers won't recognize your eye. As a eye patch. We can decorate something . . . you can make a mask for recognize . . . we could make a good mask . . . that could recognize . . .

Tommy walks over to Mike. He links his arm through his friend's and leads him over to the art table as he attempts to persuade him. "And so . . . can't recognize us. Let's make some masks, what do ya say? Alright? Now what can we do here?"

The two boys pause to look at the art materials on the table.

TOMMY: Oh, I see. Any paper on that floor?

CAREGIVER: You want some paper?

TOMMY: Yes. We want to make masks.

MIKE: To scare all the teachers and children. We got to make a mask quick.

TOMMY: And stickers too!

Each boy has a large red sheet of paper. Tommy holds a large bottle of white glue upside down, and begins making gluey lines with it on his paper.

TOMMY (*a moment later, excitedly*): Hey, look what I made, Mike! I made a Ninja Turtle! (*He adds a dollop of glue to the turtle's ear.*) I made a Ninja Turtle with numchop.

MIKE: Yeah, we're gonna . . . those are gonna be our disguises.

TOMMY (*standing back to gaze at his paper*): There's our Ninja Turtle bellywear! Hey Mike, look at the Ninja! Mike, look at my Ninja Turtle I made! Mike!

Gretchen (suddenly): I wonder how many people reading this conversation are going to throw the book down at about this point, saying, "I'm not going to read any more of that stuff."

Betty (surprised): Why would they do that?

Gretchen: Because we're talking about letting children take risks, and many adults feel strongly about their responsibility for taking care of children and keeping them safe. And that includes keeping bad feelings under wraps: "It isn't nice to talk that way. We're all friends here." If children are taught that bad feelings aren't acceptable, then they'll acquire the habit of being nice. The earlier that happens, the better.

Betty: Oh, I do think differently than that. You're reminding me how much my thinking has been influenced by the psychodynamic view that it's important to acknowledge bad feelings and help people—including children—find safe ways to express them. When this doesn't happen, they're likely to get stored up and do eventual damage, to oneself or to others. "Using your words" instead of your fists is one of the safe ways to express feelings.

Gretchen: So are painting and clay and play dough. So is pretend play.

Play is important for children partly because it offers symbolic ways of dealing with strong feelings. They can't hurt baby sisters, but they can spank the doll. They can't keep earthquakes from happening, but they can be the maker of earthquakes when they're building with blocks.

Betty: I've always remembered Erikson's (1950) writing about the "macrosphere"—the big world in which children aren't in control—and the "microsphere"—what he called "the small world of manageable toys" (p. 221), where children are in charge. Such a relief, I'd think; to be a small child is to be constantly at the mercy of adults, benevolent or otherwise.

Gretchen: There you go, offending people again. "At the mercy of adults" will really distress my friends who think they're good for children.

Betty: I know some of your friends, and they *are* good for children. But sometimes they have to make children do things for their own good, and because they're grownups and big and powerful, they can do that. Why have children—and adults—always liked fairy tales, which always have evil characters as well as good? I think of Mary Howarth's (1989) reflection on fairy tale roles as she reflects on her life as wife and mother.

> My husband had transformed himself from Frog to Prince and back again to Frog innumerable times. Also I had watched myself change from Princess to Witch, to Wicked Stepmother, and back to Good Queen in a space of 24 hours, so I knew that also could happen. . . . Perhaps fairy tales contained truths that were healthy for children to experience. (p. 58)

Why have children always played good guys/bad guys? Pretending to be powerful is one of children's most compelling play themes, as the creators and sellers of media dramas know very well. Media dramas have great attraction for many children because they offer roles and scripts to be re-created in play with oneself as hero.

Gretchen: But adults—my friends, anyway—don't like media violence. I hate it, when I'm teaching preschool. I want them to play nicely, not run around shooting and kicking at each other.

Betty: Then why were you so accepting when Tommy zapped you? You joined right into the play?

Gretchen: Well, as I said before, I really was the enemy; I was intruding on their play with a video camera, and I deserved to be zapped. This wasn't the only time in my research that I worried about being an intruder, and Tommy and Mike gave me the chance to acknowledge that playfully.

I also keep being aware, as I observe in child care, how constant is the supervision under which we keep children. Young children at home have many more opportunities for privacy, while adults are busy doing other things. Their time is less planned, and they have more time to play—unless, of course, they're just plopped in front of the TV.

Betty: Those teachers who think children are better off in good child care than at home must have visions of constant TV—and I suppose they're right to some degree.

Gretchen: Or else they're people who don't value children's play as a learning activity and think a teacher-directed curriculum is more desirable. But crowd control is among the constant issues in child care, just because there are many more children than adults and it's important not to let out-of-bounds behavior escalate. You noticed that the boys' caregiver stopped the play, even though I was permitting and even encouraging it?

Betty: Yes, she simply interrupted it to enforce rules about hurting—even pretend hurting. Do you know why?

Gretchen: Well, she was the responsible adult, while I was only a visitor. It was her job to keep the children physically and emotionally safe; and in this particular school community, she also is expected to teach a philosophy of nonviolence. She didn't encourage "bad play" as defined by the program. I could.

Betty: "Bad play" is defined differently in different programs, isn't it? I suspect this reflects not only adults' values and expectations but also their fears: If this gets too chaotic will I lose control? Will someone get hurt? Will people think I'm a bad teacher?

Gretchen: This caregiver got anxious when the play was physical, but she helped the kids find mask-making materials "to scare all the teachers and children." That wouldn't be acceptable either if this were a program where the value "We are all friends here" was continually emphasized.

Betty: This program certainly values friendship, but staff don't believe you can legislate feelings. So it's OK to be mad, or to feel mean, but there are limits to how feelings can be acted out. (Those limits probably vary with different staff members and at different times.) Children aren't allowed to shoot people—although I'm sure they do sometimes, when an adult doesn't see them. On the other hand, their creativity in inventing other ways to "get the bad guys" is appreciated and supported.

Gretchen: It's even modeled. Right after Dave pretended to fall over Tommy's rope trap, this is what happened.

TICKLERS

Pausing thoughtfully, Tommy says: "Oh, that's what I gotta have. I do have to have that." He walks over and stands in front of Dave, who kneels down to be at Tommy's level.

TOMMY: What do you think I want to have?

DAVE: I don't know, what?

TOMMY: Remember last night I um, you know . . .

DAVE: Oh, that story that I told?

TOMMY: Yeah, the Halloween one. You need a feather to tickle . . .

DAVE: Right . . . oh, to tickle the guys? Well, let's look around the yard. You know what, I think I saw some feathers in the yard the other day from one of the birds. If we look real hard, we can find one.

TOMMY: And I need some honey.

DAVE: Well, we can make-believe honey. We can get some sand and that can be honey. And what else did he do? He tickled one, and he put honey on the other one, and what else?

Overhearing, Mike acts the answer. He points the end of a rope in front of his face and makes a spraying sound.

DAVE: Sprayed him with a hose!

TOMMY (*taking the nozzle end of the hose out from under the porch and showing it to Dave*): We could have it and pretend water could come out. Here, why don't we use this one?

DAVE: You can use that one and I'll see if I can find you a feather somewhere, alright?

Betty: What was that about?

Gretchen: I asked Dave afterwards, during an interlude.

It's a story I made up. I have to make up a story everyday. See, we were telling ghostbuster stories so we're doing nonviolent ones now. I made up this character, the first one, his name is "Ropes." And he uses his words and he uses a rope to lasso the guys . . . to have the bad guys taken to jail. But he does not use his fists or a gun. See, that's what they wanted, guns and knives. And I said "Nope." So he uses a rope and he uses his words. They play these stories every day. (D. Tolbert, personal communication, October 12, 1989)

Dave's story expressed a particular political position; through it he intended to teach against violence in hopes of affecting children's attitudes about war play.

Betty: That's amazing. So many adults just lose their perspective and sense of humor when they feel children are violating their values. Stern forbidding is effective for some behaviors by children but not for others; I've never seen it work in banning superhero play. Kids just get sneaky —

which is, of course, a necessary survival skill for kids trapped in a world of adults.

Gretchen: Sneaky? People don't want kids to be sneaky.

Betty: Sorry—that's a loaded word. But kids do keep finding ways to meet their needs even when adults don't approve. In every program I've ever been in that bans shooting, including those in which I've taught, children shoot. But having become aware of adults' feelings, they often avoid shooting while adults are watching. And if they're seen, they reassure adults that nothing bad is going on: "It's not a gun, teacher. Don't be scared." It's teachers, not kids, who are scared of pretend guns.

Gretchen: Because kids know how to pretend, while many adults have forgotten how? That makes sense.

Betty: Dave certainly hasn't forgotten how. He obviously has decided, "If you can't beat 'em, join 'em," and he uses his remarkable imagination and humor to invite them into *his* play, which picks up on their power theme but is even more interesting than their play.

Gretchen: Children do need adults as play models, some of the time. The idea of co-opting superhero play by complicating it comes up in several things I've read (Carlsson-Paige & Levin, 1987; Gronlund, 1992; Paley, 1984), and I like it. It emphasizes adults' influence as play models or facilitators, while acknowledging the importance of *power* issues to many children. What children need to deal with, they play.

Betty: How come it's boys who do most of the superhero play? Isn't power an issue for girls?

Gretchen: Remember how Paley (1984) talks, in *Boys and Girls: Superheroes in the Doll Corner*, about girls exerting power in other ways, like making an enclosure and trying to keep everyone else out of it? "Only *beautiful* princesses can play here." Girls are apt to talk more, boys to act.

Betty: What I remember from that book is Paley's description of girls domesticating the boys' play—like feeding the invading lion and putting him to bed.

Gretchen: Or you can go all the way back to Erikson's (1950) psychoanalytic description of boys' and girls' block play: Boys build towers, girls build enclosures.

Betty: Can't you have strategies for getting power other than trapping and zapping?

Gretchen: Like what?

Betty: Like building a nest—a safe haven, an enclosure, a house—and going inside and locking the door. Women have always done that. So have men; think of castles and forts. You don't have to zap the bad guys as long as you can keep them out of your territory.

Gretchen: Oh. Did you see the observation of Tommy and Mike in which the traps turned into beds? Here it is.

A DIFFERENT KIND OF TRAP

Amicably, Tommy, Mike, and Zeke come into the house from the yard. They go directly to the cubby area, where Mike sits down to take off his sandals. Pulling off his tennis shoes, Tommy announces, "This is a shoe off game." Zeke answers, "I don't know how to get these off. It's too hard for children."

Both Tommy and Mike try to help Zeke untie his laces. Tommy holds Zeke's foot in his lap and works on the shoes with concentration. Tommy shouts excitedly, "I got it, I got it, I got it!" Meanwhile Mike begins collecting pillows and blankets. Feeling friendly, he tells the video maker, "We're making a different kind of trap."

Mike is arranging blankets on the floor in the main room. Joan has been solicited to untie Zeke's shoes. After doing so she says, "I need to ask you, Mike. You're making a trap? Keep the trap over here because this is a walkway where people come in and out. So make it to this edge of this floor."

MIKE (*listens attentively and then resumes his task*): I'm making my bed.

TOMMY: First this will be my bed.

MIKE (*pointing*): That's my bed, not yours.

JOAN: Mike, if I can push this over a little bit, over against the wall . . .

MIKE: Why?

JOAN: Because this is a walkway and people are coming in . . . there.

TOMMY (*brings out a one-piece beach chair for Mike*): Here's something you need to make a bed! Here's a bed, Mike. That's a thing you lay on a bed.

Mike tries several different arrangements with the beach chair. Tommy goes to his cubby and pulls out a bundle of blankets, hauling them out to the main room. Joan reminds him to leave the pathway to the door clear. At the foot of Mike's bed, Tommy spreads out a large green pillow, a white blanket, and then a quilt, announcing, "There's my bed." As he returns to the cubby area, he informs Zeke, "I made my bed!"

"I made mine!" responds Zeke. "This one's mine!"

"This one's mine!" Tommy hops onto his blankets, peels them apart and crawls down inside of them, saying, "This is my cozy one. I won't see my eyes."

Tommy covers himself from head to toe. One of the boys suggests turning off the lights. Tommy says, "Yeah, I'll turn them off." He climbs out from under the blankets and flicks the nearby light switch. As soon as Tommy has his back turned, a boy teasingly turns them back on. Mike says, "Don't! Stop!" He jumps up to turn them off. The boy switches them on, and Joan intervenes.

MIKE: We want the lights off because we are tired and we want to go to sleep. We're trying to get a little sleep.

JOAN: Okay, what I can suggest to you . . .

BOY: And I want the light on.

JOAN: . . . is I also need to have the light on. But if you want to be in a place where the lights are off, you can move your beds back into the dress-up area. That's where you can turn the lights off.

TOMMY: Okay, we'll take our stuff in there. Let's make our beds all over.

Tommy, Mike, and Zeke haul their things to an enclosed area at the back of the room. As the three boys rearrange their bedding, the boy knocks on the window of the room. Tommy warns, "Quit knocking at the door, chuzbutt!"

Betty: I'm fascinated. Do superheroes have to reassure themselves that they're building traps before they can play being little kids at naptime? Do they have to keep up their trapper reputation? Even trappers need a little sleep. . . .

Gretchen: These three boys, I learned, were in Dave's nap group, and Dave told them them the "Ropes" stories at naptime. Naptime in this program is usually a pleasant experience for every child, and it is understandable that children would think to simulate it in play. The staffing is configured so that the schedules of the morning and afternoon teachers overlap, enabling every teacher to participate in the naptime routine. The cots are grouped in pods, and each child rests with his or her primary caregiver and the same group of friends everyday. So Tommy, Zeke, and Mike are used to sleeping together because Dave is their primary caregiver. It is an unspoken naptime ritual to spend time arranging blankets, pillows, and stuffed animals in order to "make [the] beds all over."

Betty: I was really struck, watching these boys, by their high level of mutuality during this observation. Even getting Zeke's shoe untied was a challenge each of them worked to solve. Their recent experiences with ropes and knot tying in the yard were not unrelated, and may have made this problem an interesting one! To sustain cooperative social interactions is a challenge for two children—cooperative play among three is more difficult and requires each player's skill in keeping it satisfying for all.

Gretchen: Each boy's involvement seemed sustained by a common interest in the play script: naptime. For master players, knotted shoelaces are minor interruptions that do not interfere with play.

Betty: They were building solidarity by re-creating one of the settings in which they're together every day. And placing one's bed is a good way to establish territory, isn't it? Especially in child care, where a child's cubby and his cot are the only spaces designated as his. Everything else has to be shared. I noticed that each child made it clear, in some way, that "this is my bed, not yours."

Gretchen: It was very realistic play, in spite of the "trap" announcement. They took off their shoes, laid out their beds in the middle of the classroom (which is what the caregivers do at naptime), turned off the lights (as the caregivers do at naptime), and snuggled into their cozy beds.

Betty: But it wasn't naptime. And so the caregiver intervened twice to set limits: You can't have a trap in the middle of the public walkway, and you can't have the lights off during play time. That seems reasonable.

Gretchen: No, it wasn't — because they were pretending it was naptime, and those things do happen during naptime.

Betty: But grownups, not children, are in charge of the schedule. It wasn't naptime, and other people were moving around the space. I thought Joan was much more supportive of the play than many caregivers would be. She was setting limits that not only protected others from what the boys had announced was a trap, but also protected the boys' play from others. First she just asked them to move out of the walkway. Later she told them if they wanted to have a private place with the lights off, to go to the dress-up area. As I recall, that's a little walled-off alcove just right for a bedroom.

Gretchen: Yes, it is. And they accepted her suggestions in the spirit in which they were offered. She was consistent but respectful; she listened to their needs but also made others' needs clear to them.

Betty: It helped, I think, that she presented the problem to them in an interestingly democratic way. Her idea for a compromise was prefaced with the words, "I can suggest to you," which had the effect of leaving the solution to the problem with the boys.

Gretchen: And she intervened to problem solve, as well, when lights off/lights on became an issue with another child. But don't you think they could have handled that one, if she hadn't?

Betty: Yes, I do, although they might have solved it less peaceably. These are such competent 4-year-old master players! They know how to be friends, construct a play setting, and play out an interesting idea.

CHAPTER 4

Dennis: Territoriality

Gretchen: The next child we are going to observe, Dennis, challenged my resolve to videotape more than any other. I quickly learned from Dennis the meaning of the "rejecting" behaviors in the Child's Mode of Behavior code (Prescott et al., 1975). When he spotted me in the yard the first time with the camera, his immediate response was to flee! He climbed down inside a large hollow box that had been set up as part of an obstacle course by a teacher. Declaring that he and Peter were playing house, Dennis claimed it as his own. When the teacher told them it was intended for everybody, Dennis and Peter went indoors, with me close at their heels. Dennis protested when he saw me, "Don't take a picture." Then he scrunched down underneath a block shelf and peeked out to see if I had taken the hint.

Betty: It sounds as if the presence of the camera interfered with the boys' play.

Gretchen (nodding): I learned that while I might wish to be invisible, I obviously was not!

Betty: It occurs to me that middle-class kids may be more accustomed to having control over the adults in their lives than children from working-class backgrounds. Did you get more negative reactions to your videoing in the Children's School than at the state preschools?

Gretchen: Oh, yes! At the Children's School Dennis was clearly communicating that he would not immediately oblige my wish to film his play. And you saw how Tommy and Mike felt about the camera in their yard. Another time at the Children's School, after I had filmed Roger several times and was virtually ignored, he abruptly stopped what he was doing, turned to me, and asked, "Why do you keep following us?"

In the state preschools, several children even expressed an interest in the camera. They asked to look through the lens and wanted to know if they could view the "movies" I was making on the school's video monitor. Taisha one morning spent a long time creating a display of *all* the dolls. It was a wonderful assortment. Then she sat down among them, folded her arms, and said, "Now take a picture."

A 3-year-old newcomer to one of the state programs, José was working on getting comfortable in the busy routine of preschool. I filmed him only for a couple of minutes several times because he would look away, turn his back, or walk toward a far corner of the room. A nosey video camera was not in José's best interests!

Betty: What are these differences about, do you think?

Gretchen: I expect that children from working-class backgrounds are taught that polite behavior toward teachers includes not saying anything that might be considered disrespectful. In higher-income groups, many families and teachers value children's ability to question authority and assert their rights. At the time I had to think about my own behavior as camera person. I did not want to be insensitive to the needs of the less vocal children or intimidated by the assertiveness of the outspoken kids.

Betty: Some children are more bothered by intrusions than others. In settings that offer them no privacy, I suppose such children avoid involvement or give up easily, resigned to the fact that privacy is not to be had.

Gretchen: Yes, and I cared that in my role I not become so invasive that the sense of privacy that was available in the environments at both the state schools and the Children's School would be undermined.

The preschool program at the Children's School at Pacific Oaks is a morning program for forty 3-, 4-, and 5-year-olds. The children attend separate programs for the first part of the morning; they are divided into a younger and an older group. One master teacher each and several other teachers and students work with the children during small-group time. The groups merge for free play, during which children choose among various equipment and activities both indoors and out. The program resides in the downstairs of a two-story, California-style bungalow, with a big, sweeping porch.

The next time I filmed Dennis, he found some ways of coping with the camera. Dennis is 3 years, 8 months old, a Euro-American child with a head of tousled brown hair. Dennis's teacher described him as rambunctious, assertive, rowdy, and spirited, adding that he enjoyed playing adventure themes. This time, like Tommy, he played that I was the enemy. But Dennis did not use zapping and trapping. He would run to a hiding place, and when he felt safe he would look out at me.

SEEKING PRIVACY

The Ninja Turtles—Dennis, Peter, and Roger—are running toward their hideout. It is two large hollow boxes with open sides that have been placed facing each other. (They were built for the yard by a parent—each is approximately 5′ × 3′ × 3′.) The boxes are separated by a 1′-wide crack to allow for easy entry and lots of privacy inside for several children.

Dennis's arms are outstretched in front of him. Peter calls, "I got two pizzas," and Dennis responds, "I got lots of 'em!"

The three boys sit down inside the box, pretending to eat pizza. I move in closer, hoping to record their dialogue. Grinning, Dennis and the others look up. They dash out the backside of the box, bespeaking a shared understanding that the camera is the enemy. Dennis yells, "Yikes, she's gonna film us!"

The boys settle down inside a different box and have a conversation. Seeming distracted by the camera, Dennis runs back to the large boxes and yells, "Come on, guys, let's go."

Peter and Roger return to the main hideout; they have a brief discussion, inaudible to the camera. Soon, with a small pink blanket in his hands, Dennis emerges. As if guarding the hideout, he looks around. He grins at the camera twice. Then he climbs on top of the box, sits down cross-legged, looks at the camera again, shakes open the blanket, and covers himself completely. Dennis sits absolutely still for a few moments. Peeking out, he grins at the camera and ducks under the blanket again. Moments later, just as Roger and Peter are emerging from the box, Dennis uncovers himself and stands tall.

ROGER (*pointing at Dennis*): There's Donatello.

PETER: Are you trapped?

DENNIS: No.

ROGER: Oh, yes, you are. (*Dennis wiggles his body and swings his arms.*)

PETER: Did you be off?

DENNIS: Cut. I *cut* the rope.

PETER: Come on, Donatello.

DENNIS (*jumping down*): Our bomb!

Dennis climbs up to the top of the box again, and stands there briefly. Jumping to the ground, he remembers that the camera is the enemy, and yells, "Yikes." He runs in a large circle across the yard and hides behind a tree. Meanwhile, Roger and Peter are straddling a log, pretending to drive a vehicle. Dennis quickly joins them, sitting down behind Roger.

Betty: Clearly this is master play by Dennis and the turtles! Dennis was able to accommodate the camera when it could be integrated as the enemy into his play script. In play he could taunt it, flee from it, and escape it, symbolically at least. He had figured out a friendly and playful way to deal with a major intrusion that sometimes even tried to penetrate sewer hideaways.

Gretchen: Yes, Dennis really pulled one over on me when he covered himself with the blanket. He looked out from under it and grinned right at the camera. He seemed to be conveying a double meaning: He was playing Donatello in a rope trap but he was also saying, "Hey, Camera, under here I can hide from you." He seemed quite pleased with himself!

Betty: I think Dennis had figured out that you were not going to impose school rules, and knew that it was safe to playfully test your authority as an adult.

Gretchen: When we were coding the behaviors, using the Child's Mode of Behavior (Prescott et al., 1975), we found we often scored Dennis's behavior as copes effectively with social constraints (I1b).

Betty: Explain, please.

Gretchen: I think my presence was a social constraint for Dennis. And play was a safe way for Dennis to communicate his feelings about the video camera. In play he could safely say, "I can deal with you, Camera, by giving you the role of enemy (because that is what you are) and by asserting my desire for privacy." Tommy dealt with me by zapping and shooting, but there is little tolerance for this behavior in most preschool programs, and many children would not risk being this openly hostile in their behavior toward adults.

Betty: I agree. Dennis was learning to assert himself in ways that he knew would not offend. The truly autonomous child is one who can express his feelings and get his needs met while taking into account the needs of other people.

Gretchen: Well, most of the time adults aren't around with video cameras on their shoulders, thank heavens.

Betty: I am so impressed with Dennis's competence in inventing symbols to express meaning. If we were not watching closely it would have been easy to overlook or misunderstand what he was doing when he enacted escaping from the rope trap. And early in the video, when he runs across the yard with his arms outstretched—it wasn't hard to figure out that he was carrying a large pizza!

Gretchen: This is one of the ways master players sustain and elaborate the illusion of play: enacting carrying a pizza or escaping a rope trap or whatever, is "read" by the other players, who "reply" by acting and speaking in keeping with the script.

Betty: Physical gestures are just one of the languages of children's play. Words are another. Should teachers try to teach children to do this kind of pretending?

Gretchen: I think of all the fingerplays and songs that encourage children to use gesture to convey meaning. And I observed a teacher using little pretend gestures at cleanup time. She was making engine sounds and "driving" miniature cars to the toy box just the way children will when they're playing. Beginning players are enchanted when adults behave this way. It seems to me it's like learning a language—if the child is interested in dramatic play when she is 2 or 3 (and what child isn't?), she'll learn it by watching and reading adults' gestures and by paying attention to other children's dramatic play.

Betty: I'm thinking how really complex children's dramatic play becomes and how creative their symbolic expression can be. To appreciate its complexity one can observe it closely and follow its unfolding. It's a form of storytelling; the preschool child's most natural way of telling a story is to play it.

Gretchen: A code we found ourselves scoring frequently in the master player study was attends-with-concentration-to-the-activity (I2). We noticed how children would return to the same script again and again, even after major interruptions like nap or going home for the night. What interested me was that the play was never a replication of earlier play—it seemed more like the next episode. It was as if they were into the next chapter. The children seemed very motivated to elaborate and evolve their play in this way.

Betty: It's useful to think of dramatic play as the developmental precursor to storytelling. Adults *tell* stories rather than act them, and for stories in the dramatic form, they go to the theatre or a take in a movie.

Gretchen: In another observation, a teacher intervenes to encourage David, a younger child, to join the "Batman" play of Dennis and friends. Her intervention is not particularly effective for David, but Dennis responds to it with a generous suggestion that David play the Joker.

INCLUDING OTHERS

Dennis, Peter, and Shawna, who is wearing a black-and-red Batman shirt, are gathered on the porch around a toy catalog. They are laughing at Peter's suggestions for silly names for some of the toys: "Snow Batmobile! That's pretty by-got-coo-kie!"

As if to signal time for play, Dennis jumps up and dashes down into the yard. Shawna and Peter follow.

The teacher, Barbara, asks, "Hey Dennis, hey Shawna, could you help me move some blocks?"

Dennis runs around to a four-rung ladder, which is leaning against a large wooden cable spool. There are three large hollow blocks placed vertically on the top of the spool. As Dennis climbs, David approaches the ladder. Dennis reaches over and pushes at David to stay clear of the ladder. Barbara has been watching.

BARBARA: Dennis, you can tell David, "I'm climbing, please don't."

DENNIS: I'm climbing.

PETER: Can I climb after you, Dennis?

BARBARA (*as Dennis climbs up on top of the hollow blocks*): I'm going to move these blocks because I'm not comfortable. I think they're too tippy when you're up that high. (*She takes two blocks off the top of the spool where Dennis is standing. Dennis carefully tosses the third one to the ground. Peter now is climbing up the ladder.*)

DENNIS: Peter, let's play Batman. I'm Robin, and you're Batman . . .

PETER (*sounding certain*): I'm not playing Batman.

DENNIS (*calling to Shawna*): Hey, you wanna play Batman?

PETER: Okay, I'll play Batman, Dennis.

DAVID (*now standing on the spool beside Peter and Dennis*): And I do!

BARBARA: David does. And David does.

DENNIS (*pointing to Shawna*): You be Batlady and I'll be Robin and you be Batman.

PETER: No, I'm Batman.

BARBARA (*reminding them*): And David does.

DENNIS (*pointing at Shawna and at David in turn*): And you're Batlady. And you're Joker.

DAVID (*cautiously, in a small voice*): No, I'm Alie.

BARBARA: You're who, David? You said just a minute ago you were going to be somebody. Dennis wants to hear who you're going to be. You need to stand up and talk to the kids when you play with them, and then they'll know what you want to play. You really want to play, but you're kind of thinking about it?

Dennis and Peter are listening to Barbara's concerns. Then Dennis turns, jumps to the ground, and calls, "Come on, guys!" Running across to Shawna, Dennis calls, "Come on, Batlady!" She and Peter chase Dennis as he runs around the yard.

Back at the spool, Dennis calls, "On the batmobile!" He climbs up the ladder carefully.

BARBARA (*to David*): Here they come. The batmobile! David's manning the batmobile. Here's Dennis. Here's Peter.

DENNIS: Here's Robin!

BARBARA: Who's Robin? Are you pretending David's Robin?

DENNIS: No, I'm Robin, and he's Joker (*pointing to David*), and she's Batlady.

PETER: Yeah, and I'm Batman!

BARBARA: Joker!

DENNIS (*continues*): And Batman and Robin punch!

BARBARA: They punch? Why do they need to punch?

DENNIS (*swinging his arms*): They have to kill bad guys.

BARBARA: You know, I've watched Batman and I've never seen him kill anybody. They capture. They have those special things to capture people.

DENNIS: That's why they punch. (*He pretends to punch his own belly.*)

BARBARA: Sometimes they do punch. Would you make sure if you want to play that way that someone understands it's a game and that the game is okay? Dennis?

David asks Barbara about her glasses. Dennis and Peter listen briefly as she explains why she wears glasses.

Dennis is on the edge of the top of the spool, with Peter nearby. In mock fear, Dennis says, "Yikes, the sharks are gonna get me." As if he is avoiding sharks, Dennis takes a stretching, cautious step from the lower edge of the spool to a large hollow block nearby.

BARBARA (*realizing that it's cleanup time*): Okay, I need help with blocks. I'd say Batman is strong enough for that.

DENNIS: You know, I am tough.

BARBARA: You're tough? Dennis, are you strong enough to carry some blocks for me? Thank you. One at a time? Two at a time? (*Dennis reaches over and takes two large hollow blocks, one in each hand.*)

BARBARA: Oh, can you really do two at a time?

Dennis walks toward the block shed, dragging two triangular-shaped blocks. Turning, he grins directly at the camera and sticks out his tongue. "No filming me!"

Gretchen agrees. "Okay, I'll turn it off. Thanks, Dennis." Dragging two blocks, Dennis walks to the block shed.

Gretchen: This is a Batman who is happy to display his prowess even at cleanup time!

Betty: I was thinking about Barbara's attempts to involve David. He was quite reticent to join in, wasn't he? When Dennis offered him a part — Joker, the bad guy — he refused it; and when Barbara tried to help he successfully diverted her attention from the dramatic play to a conversation about glasses. I wonder if he was intimidated by the play and ambivalent about his wish to get into it — or simply more interested in conversation with an adult.

Gretchen: My sense is that a vocal adult with an agenda of her or his own interrupts children's dramatic play. Is it okay for a teacher to intervene on behalf of a less skilled player if it interrupts other children's play?

Betty: Vivian Paley (1992) certainly thinks so. I'm not sure what I think. Barbara was trying to show David how to get into the play, but he undermined her efforts. Her efforts seemed awkward to me, as if she didn't know quite what to do or say. That's a common experience for teachers; children are often a jump ahead of us. I was a bit confused by Barbara's request for help in moving blocks. The first time, was she suggesting a task to divert running children?

Gretchen: I think so. It was nearly cleanup time and perhaps it made more sense to her at that point to get them interested in a task than to allow the dramatic play to become too engrossing. Although she did seem to think it was valuable to take a few minutes to get David interested in the play.

Betty: Some children can benefit by direct help from an adult ("play training") in learning skills for sociodramatic play. One play training approach is to model or encourage a child to play a role the adult is familiar with by suggesting the words and/or the action he might use. Smilansky (1968) found this worked quite successfully with beginning players.

Gretchen: And indirectly Barbara was suggesting to Dennis and company that they might discover interesting children to play with outside of their usual cluster of friends.

Betty: I was very interested when Barbara asserted that she had watched Batman and she had never seen him kill anybody. Like Dave, Barbara was a teacher with a peace agenda who used the context of the child's play to express her own concerns about violent behavior.

Gretchen: I noticed that she did not try to discourage or stop the superhero theme. Vivian Paley's (1984) Darth Vader quote is one to keep in mind.

> If I have not yet learned to love Darth Vader, I have at least made some useful discoveries while watching him at play. As I interrupt less, it becomes clear that boys' play is serious drama, not morbid mischief. Its rhythms and images are often discordant to me, but I must try to make sense of a style that, after all, belongs to half the population of the classroom. (p. xii)

Betty: Both Vivian Paley and Barbara are experienced, confident teachers not easily intimidated by children's play, and are clear that it isn't real, it's just pretend. When Barbara asked Dennis to let other children know that "Batman" was just a game, she was reminding him that he had control over his play.

Gretchen: And giving him something else to think about—that in this community of children some people might not be as enchanted by superhero play as he was, and they might even be frightened by it!

Betty: Children's superhero play is probably motivated by a need to understand such powerful and frightening images as killing and capturing. We discussed this in regard to Tommy's zapping and trapping play (Chapter 3). Adults—especially nice female teachers—often are frightened by these images too, and threatened when they appear and persist in the play of children (especially assertive 4-year-old boys). Yet they're usually aware that forbidding this kind of play doesn't work; it just goes underground so as not to scare the teachers!

Gretchen: We always get back to the importance of taking children's play seriously, don't we? Play is children's way of confronting the issues in their real and fantasy lives. Let's do the last Dennis observation now.

PLANNING AS PLAY

Dennis is sitting outside the edge of the sandbox with Greg and Sean. They are using small plastic shovels to scoop sand into a paddle wheel sand toy. There are several large rubber dinosaurs scattered around them.

DENNIS: Big, big pile, right? Right, Greg?

GREG: Right. They're goin' big hole.

SEAN: No, we're not doing that.

DENNIS: No. No.

GREG: Right?

DENNIS: Right.

GREG: We're playing Batman, right?

SEAN: Right.

GREG: This is our cave for the Joker. Right?

DENNIS: Right, Joker.

GREG: I'm Batman, right? Hey, I know what. We're gonna be two Batmans. Yeah. We're putting dirt right here, right?

DENNIS: We're making a big, big pile of dirt.

GREG: Yeah, right? Yeah, for our dinosaurs.

DENNIS: Yeah, dinosaurs. (*Greg leaves with three dinosaurs and a shovel in his arms.*)

SEAN (*in response to Roger, who has approached with a handful of sand*): We don't need any help! No.

ROGER (*putting sand into the paddle wheel*): I wanted to. (*He walks away.*)

DENNIS (*calling after him*): Yeah, you can help! It's time for shoveling!

(*Roger does not return.*)

Dennis stands up with the paddle wheel in his arms. The others retrieve the dinosaurs and shovels. They carry their things and settle down in a more secluded spot behind the storage shed. Arranging the dinosaurs carefully around them, Dennis, Greg, and Sean resume their digging.

GREG: That could be Little Foot. That could be Little Foot, right?

DENNIS (*pointing to a small dinosaur*): That could be Little Foot!

GREG (*chanting*): That could be Little Foot. That could be Little Foot!

DENNIS: You know Shark-tooth killed the mother.
GREG: And this one goes wham, wham, wham!

While Dennis watches, Greg pours sand into the paddle wheel from his cupped hand.

Betty: At the beginning it seemed like exploratory play for Dennis, not Batman this time. But Greg insisted on Batman. (Is he someone who usually gets to play Batman with Dennis, or was this his chance?) Dennis was mildly agreeable—"Right, Joker"—but his real interest was "making a big, big pile of dirt." Greg switches the dramatic theme to dinosaurs, which are right there in the environment, but even that doesn't grab Dennis until Greg mentions Little Foot. What appeared to be physical play really may have been master builders preparing a "big pile of dirt" that was to become the scene for dramatic play with miniatures—in this case using dinosaurs, instead of their own bodies, to play the story of "Little Foot."

Gretchen: The drama of power—Batman, dinosaurs—does seem endlessly fascinating to some children. Teachers often prefer dinosaurs to superheroes, don't they? But both can go "wham, wham, wham," in Greg's words.

Betty: I liked the conscious thinking-about-thinking that's going on here. The boys are planning the play—they're negotiating the script and know that's what they're doing. Wouldn't verbal planning be a form of master building?

Gretchen: Yes, of course—they're verbally constructing their play! I think children do a lot of this and probably teachers are aware of it but don't recognize it as planning because we think of planning as serious business. But it's play that engages children, and it makes sense that children will discuss what is on their minds.

Betty: "Planning as serious business" reminds me of the way the High/Scope curriculum introduces a planning time as the first activity of the morning, to encourage children to make decisions before they actually begin to play. But when I've watched preschool children doing teacher-initiated "planning," it seems to be just a ritual to get through before the teacher will let them go play. I think this is premature for preoperational children, who most often plan by doing. That's in contrast to children becoming concrete operational, in the primary grades, for whom "make a plan for your project" is an increasingly significant challenge.

Gretchen: Here we're seeing master players whose verbal construction of the play is self-initiated and seems as satisfying as play itself. Planning as play: I like that! The boys were competent when they could make plans about what mattered to them: their fantasy play.

Betty: It's interesting to me how this time *no one* took notice of the camera. They were immersed in concerns of their own. Moments of privacy like this support solidarity among peers.

Gretchen: I love the quote in Fein (1987), where she says, "If dramatic play is to happen, it must be between friends and in private, secluded places" (p. 270).

CHAPTER 5

Sharon: Manageable Small Worlds

CREATING PLEASING PATTERNS

Sharon is sitting on the carpeted floor near Georgia, her teacher, and three other children who are building with blocks. Although she is the same size as all the other children, Sharon is 5 years old and eligible for kindergarten. Because Sharon has thrived in this state-sponsored pre-school, she is attending for a second year. She is an African-American child with close-cropped hair.

Sharon has arranged three rubber Hereford cows and a calf in a neat line. She trots a brown horse to a place in the animal line-up. She retrieves two colts from behind a boy, then walks over to the cupboard to get more animals, stepping carefully around another child's construction. In the moment while she is gone, a boy scoops up her stack of animals in his arms, seemingly without mal-intent, and then leaves them in a heap on the floor. When Sharon returns, she frowns at the heap but says nothing. She tosses the three horses she is holding onto the pile. Sharon picks out a zebra and a cow, gathers three cows and a calf in her arms, and walks over to the cupboard with them. With one cow in her right hand and another in her left, she holds them facing each other and makes them "dance" on their hind legs. Glancing at the camera, she turns and begins lining up cows along the countertop. She turns a third cow belly-up to look at its udder. She looks for udders on two other cows. Then she returns to the pile of animals on the floor, picking up an armful of elephants.

Georgia speaks to Sharon about removing the animals from the countertop. Sharon "walks" two elephants down the side of the cupboard and into a box on the floor. She hangs the two large elephants by their trunks on the edge of the box, as if they are feeding. Then, in a similar fashion, she trots the other animals one by one off the counter and down into the box.

This task complete, Sharon next takes two elephants out of the box and stands them together on the floor. She places a cow, a baby elephant, and another cow in the original line. She picks up a second small elephant and tucks it between the two large elephants. She goes back to the pile of animals and selects two lions to add to her line. Carefully she places a brown horse between the lions. A zebra is next, followed by a calf and two giraffes.

Now all the animals are standing side by side in a line facing the camera, like a very wide parade. Pausing to admire her work, Sharon smiles at Georgia, who is talking to another child and doesn't see. Sharon looks up at the camera and grins. Then she gets two horses and a zebra, clasps them together in a horse-and-zebra hug, and places them carefully at the end of the line.

Charlie reaches for one of the elephants. Georgia speaks to him in Spanish, then says to Sharon in English, "Sharon, they need one to put inside their block building." Sharon takes two giraffes from the line and hands them to him. "Thank you," he says. Georgia says, playfully: "Oh, did you hear what he said?" Smiling, Sharon offers him several more animals. She smiles at the camera. Then she delivers animals around: one to Donna, one to Georgia, one to Frederick, and another one, for Georgia's lap. This is an entirely new game.

Betty: Since we've been talking about dramatic play in the other observations, I had to shift gears in looking at this play. It isn't dramatic, is it, except in brief moments of trotting and dancing and hugging?

Gretchen: Yes, you're right. This is Sharon as "master patterner" rather than "master dramatist" (Wolf & Gardner, 1979). What she's doing is constructing sets of animals — as a thoughtful child might create a painting: Let me see, what color shall I use? I like red. I'll put a red line here . . . and another red line here . . . and then I'll put a short yellow line between them . . . and a yellow sun up here in the corner . . .

Betty: It's definitely play; she's inventing the categories as she goes along. Some of her animal families are "racially mixed"; the baby elephant is placed with two cows, a horse is placed between two lions, or with two zebras. She seems to be branching out from her original cow family, using aesthetic rather than biological criteria.

Gretchen: Oh, I like that. It alerts me to the real contrast between Sharon's play and the teacher's work with another child, which was going on just before Sharon began playing with the animals. Georgia was using the animals to "teach classification skills," she told me. This was a game to be played by the adult's rules; the correct response was to group animals by species. By this criterion, Sharon was doing it "wrong."

Betty: She's playing, elaborating as she goes. She begins conventionally enough, with the cow family, but then moves into the creation of new combinations. My guess is that Sharon would be perfectly capable of grouping the animals by species if that were the game, but has chosen to transcend those categories for her own aesthetic purposes. If I were her teacher, I'd want to know this, because there's a developmental progression from random to conventional to creative. Sharon, it appears, has matured beyond conventional, to creative.

Gretchen: Don't children acquire language in the same way? Language is also a system of categories. Learning it, children progress from random babble to imitation to construction of their own understanding of both the logic and the creative possibilities of language. Think of the word play of 5-year-olds, being silly with words whose conventional meanings they have long since mastered.

Betty: And think of how younger children construct grammar. Did I tell you about the 3-year-old whose shoes I was helping to put on, not long ago? I admired the shoes, and she said proudly, "My mama bought (pause for thought) buyed me these shoes." *Bought* is conventional, learned by imitation. *Buyed*, even though it's wrong, is a more mature achievement for this child because it indicates that she's constructing English grammar for herself and has figured out the past-tense rule of adding *ed*. (*Bought* is one of the many exceptions to the rule, and she'll relearn it later.) To succeed in school Sharon will have to match cows with cows. To sustain her creative energy and purpose she'll need, as well, to hold on to her joy in matching cows with an elephant when that's her idea.

Gretchen: Georgia told me that Sharon is a child who has experienced a great deal of disconnectedness in her family life. At the time of this observation she was living with her grandparents. Her mother was in and out of rehabilitation programs, and her father was not in the picture. In preschool, nonetheless, Sharon was a master player. Imaginative play seemed to be an "island" (Carini, 1982; Werner, 1984) that enabled her to focus and define her interests and skills. There's evidence of both in this observation. Pausing to admire her work, she smiled with pleasure. Then she smiled at Georgia, hoping to be noticed, but Georgia didn't see. So then she smiled at me and my camera. I think the work was satisfying in itself, but she would have appreciated recognition too.

Betty: Constructive play frequently results in a product, and it's gratifying to have an audience for one's creations. In preschools where an adult takes down a child's painting when it's done, the opportunity for acknowledgment is built right in, isn't it? It's hard to handle a child's painting and not say anything friendly about it. Here, though, Georgia was otherwise engaged, as teachers often must be. An alert teacher can try, out of the corner of her eye, to keep track of what's going on and when acknowledgment might be important.

Gretchen: This is a busy preschool. It is one of the state-sponsored programs housed in a separate building on the grounds of an elementary school in the heart of the low- and poverty-income neighborhoods in the city. Fifteen of the 18 children in the morning program speak Spanish at home. Georgia uses a bilingual approach in her teaching. She speaks the child's first language when interacting with an individual, but with small groups or at circle, she speaks first in Spanish. This is immediately followed by the same statement in English. The aide, Mrs. Turney, speaks in English.

Here's the next observation.

PRACTICING RECIPROCITY

Sharon is at the doll house, which has been placed on one of the tables at a level accessible to the children. She is playing with Charlie. Charlie is kneeling on the floor at the table, making motor noises as he drives a four-car Lego train nearly full of Lego people. Sharon is standing on the open side of the house. She is reaching to animate her car through the window in Charlie's direction. "This car is strange. A plane!" she says.

Sharon moves back into the house, to the top floor. She calls, "Wake up! Come down here and see my new car!" Charlie, taking several Lego people out of the house, responds, "That's my car. And that's my man. That's my car right here."

Charlie takes several people out of the house. Sharon is fitting two Lego people into a car, inside the house. She talks for them, in a continuous stream of conversation, taking multiple roles, changing the intonation of her voice to match the roles. She turns the head of the woman figure seated in the front of the car so that it is looking at the male figure in the back seat.

Some of what Sharon says is indistinguishable: "I'm talking to dis. Oh, come on, Grandma . . . it will have a good trip. The children won't never . . . Charlie not . . . You know you said too much. I go where you go. Get me off to store."

CHARLIE: Want to come to the store with?

SHARON (*poking her car through the window of the house; a figure drops out*): Oh, look. I gotta get in. See?

CHARLIE: We're going to a long ride.

SHARON: No. I going to do a long ride with my wife. And I don't want you . . .

CHARLIE (*pointing to a figure on the back of his car*): Das a man.
SHARON (*leaning over to look*): Where? You may have dis one.

Charlie imitates a car motor revving up. He lifts his Lego car up over his head. Sharon choruses Charlie's actions with a loud screeching sound, lifting her car up over her head and "flying" it across the room. In this manner she "drives" the car to a corner of the room. Charlie drives his Lego car along the top of the cupboard and calls, "The store over here, Sharon." Sharon follows him with her car.

MRS. TURNEY (*to Charlie, requesting that he take care not to step on any of the children who are working on the floor nearby*): Hey, watch where you're going.
SHARON (*grinning at Mrs. Turney*): Hey!
MRS. TURNEY: Hey, ah Charlie . . . Charlie.
SHARON: Hey! Hey! (*Mrs. Turney laughs.*)

Sharon finds a two-tier parking garage in the block-building area. She carries it over to the house and fits it inside the downstairs room, announcing, "We got a parking place, we got a parking place, yeah! A big garage." She drives her car through the door of the garage. Charlie returns to the table with his car.

SHARON (*animating a figure*): You can't park in here.
GEORGIA (*from the other side of the table, in a playful high-pitched voice*): Yes, we can park in here.
SHARON (*pausing*): The garage. We don't have enough room either.
GEORGIA (*grinning*): But I want to park in here.
SHARON (*harshly, and banging a figure on the table angrily*): Park on the street. With your wife. Your wife, too.

Charlie brings a figure over to the garage.

SHARON (*using a hand that is holding a figure to push him back*): Nope, nope. You lock it.
CHARLIE: Can I get in a garage?
SHARON: It's locked. Too late. 'Cause you didn't come, afternoon.
CHARLIE: Can I play with you?
SHARON: Nope. Arlene's my partner now.
CHARLIE: You always play with me, you know.
SHARON: I play with you, but I play with Arlene too.
CHARLIE (*as a child starts taking his car from him*): Leave it alone!
SHARON: Leave it alone!

Betty: This time Sharon is involved in clearly defined dramatic play with the people in the car. She invites Charlie's attention a couple of times, as they play next to each other; but his friendly invitation to play together — "Want to come to the store with?" "We're going to a long ride" — is emphatically rejected: "No. I going to do a long ride with my wife. And I don't want you."

Gretchen: Charlie persisted, though. And when he revved his motor and flew his car, that was too dramatic to resist, and she joined him.

Betty: Until she found a parking place. Then she shut Charlie out; and when Georgia tried to intervene, Sharon was still more adamant: "Park on the street. . . . Your wife, too."

Gretchen: Charlie tried again, still friendly: "Can I get in a garage?" No, says Sharon, staying within the play script: "It's locked. Too late. Cause you didn't come, afternoon." I thought she was masterful in her use of the play script to communicate her wish to be in charge. In the real world of the classroom Sharon has to share, because the adults are in charge; but in the play world she can keep Charlie out because the door is locked.

Betty: Did you get the impression that cooperative play is less satisfying for Sharon than solitary play?

Gretchen: I'm not sure. This is a child skilled in the creation of both constructive and dramatic play with small figures—animals, people, vehicles. In her small worlds she may be experiencing more order and manageability than she has been accustomed to find in the real world.

Betty: What else has Georgia shared about her?

Gretchen: She was the first child to come to Georgia's mind when I asked her to name master players in her classroom; Georgia was fascinated by her ability to create sustained scenarios with the doll house figures. She was a very different child this year, her second in this classroom, where she has stayed even though she is eligible for kindergarten. Early last year, during free play, she would hide in the bathroom behind the toilet yelling, "I'm gonna whip you. I'm gonna get you. I'm gonna send you to a foster home." Georgia held Sharon on her lap a great deal, and gradually she began to trust her teachers and her new school.

Betty: Sharon brings to mind for me, yet again, Erikson's (1950) description of the *microsphere*—the small world of manageable toys within which a child can be in charge, unlike the frequent helplessness a child may experience in the *macrosphere* of the real world. It's always unwise to read too much into the meanings of a child's play, but there is certainly logic in the thought that only in solitary play can Sharon be fully in charge, and that she may have more need of that than some other children do.

TAKING MULTIPLE ROLES

Sharon, Arlene, and Rosita are crouched on the floor in front of a large flannel board. Arlene and Rosita speak to one another in Spanish. Sharon does not interact with them—she is searching through the flannel-backed people figures in a plastic tub on the floor beside her. Mrs. Turney is kneeling on the floor behind the group of girls, helping Sharon.

SHARON (*finding a grown male and a young girl figure*): Where's the mom?

MRS. TURNEY: I don't know. Maybe there is no momma. They're all dad-
    dies.

SHARON (*holding up twin girls*): She goin' to school. She gonna go to
    school! Let's go to school. You gotta go to school. Two plusses two is
    eight! You gotta stop fooling around in this school!

MRS. TURNEY: Two plus two is four!

SHARON: Here we go. Two plusses two. . . . So there teacher . . . Billy
    Goat . . . Billy Goat.

Sharon leaves the flannel board and walks over to the doll house with her collection of flannel people, twin girls, a boy, and a man.

(This time Sharon takes multiple roles; she animates the figure who is speaking and changes the tone of her voice. She deepens her voice when speaking for the man; her voice is high-pitched when she is a child. In the following episode, the transcription identifies the voices of the four characters played by Sharon. In several lines it is unclear which character is speaking; these are labeled "unidentified.")

ALL: Knock knock. We climb up to the window. Yeah!

Sharon puts the figures in through the window and brings them out again. She walks around to the front of the house and sits down there in a chair, continuing in the play.

TWIN GIRLS: It's spooky. It's spooky. Sister, you afraid, every day. Father
    doesn't either, stupid.

TWIN GIRLS AND BOY: What do you call 'em stupid? You. The bigger girl,
    the biggest boy . . .

(Unidentified): Get that thing's spooky outa here. Follow the leader, stu-
    pid . . . why you call him stupid? You . . . You better go, little girl. No,
    I'm not going. I hate you.

Sharon puts a girl in a bed upstairs, a man figure on a bed in another room, and the twins in bed together. You sleep in that room. You sleep in that room.

A boy is outside the house. He puts two Fisher-Price figures into one of the rooms. As animated by Sharon, the man figure throws the two "in-truder" figures out of the house. Then, the man figure leans out the window and says, "You stupid crocodile you, you out there." The boy leaves.

ONE OF THE CHILDREN: Come on, Grandpa. Sleep here before we go back
    home.

Sharon moves the man's bed into the room where the twins are in bed.

MAN: Uh-oh. I'm scared. I'm coming there with my bed.

(Unidentified, perhaps the children): Now we not scared to death.

MAN: I'm going to work, you never have fun.

Sharon sets the male figure down on the first floor. She puts the refrigerator upstairs into the bedroom with the twins.

CHILDREN (*upstairs*): That's all right. We need a ice-box. What's in the icebox, dad? Food. Then icebox. I'm scared. I'm scared.

Sharon brings the man upstairs. He "opens" the icebox. Then she places him in the beds with the twins.

(Unidentified): Me in the bed. You don't have a bed.

(Unidentified): I'm the mom and that is the dad. I'm the mom, Daddy's the dad.

GIRL: Mom, look.

MAN: Daughter, don't say that.

GIRL: I'm gonna get me some . . . (inaudible)

(Unidentified): Go to sleep blankets.

MAN: It's in the morning, wake up, kids! Wake up.

GIRL: I don't feel good.

MAN: Well, you goin' to school.

GIRL: I don't feel good.

MAN: If you don't go to school, you'll be kicked out of school!

BOY: I'm going downstairs to get dressed.

TWINS: Always have to go to school . . .

Sharon puts the three children back in the beds. She picks up the grown male figure, saying "Stupid dad, stupid dad."

Betty: Wow! This isn't preschool, this is play therapy. Do you really think we should include it in the book?

Gretchen: Well, it happened in preschool, not with a therapist but with Sharon herself firmly in charge. It's a good reminder that play can be therapeutic in its own right, if children have toys and time and perceived privacy. A therapist might help a child with such play, if help were needed. Most teachers, I think, should simply rely on the power of the play itself.

Betty: That's a loving but firm daddy Sharon has created, isn't he—a daddy who can be depended on to keep you safe and make you do what's right?

Gretchen: Yes, indeed. And Sharon, of course, is a child who doesn't know her daddy—though her grandpa, with whom she lives, may very well be her model for good fathering. If you were Sharon's teacher and noticed this play, what would you do?

Betty: I'd stay out of it, I think, though I'd eavesdrop if I could. Certainly I'd think about it, and be glad that a child with a complex family life is such a masterful player. I'd continue to learn what I could about the family.

Gretchen: It isn't only children from unstable homes who play out night terrors, though. Nightmares are part of childhood; many children can benefit by getting them out into the light of day.

Betty: Bad dreams and other night terrors are a general topic that could be brought up by a teacher with the group, aren't they? But would you talk with Sharon about her play, if you were her teacher?

Gretchen: I might, given her evident trust of her teachers. I'd do it privately with her, because her play themes seem quite private, asking her at some other time if she'd like to tell me a story about what she was playing in the doll house. That would give her another opportunity to express it, this time with a sympathetic listener.

Betty: I like the way Vivian Paley (1990) asks children questions about their play: "'I heard you and Samantha playing kitty before'" (p. 130). I could imagine commenting to Sharon about a specific bit of her play: "I noticed you had twin girls in your house." That's an interesting fact that doesn't read any emotional content into the play and gives Sharon an invitation to conversation if she'd like.

Gretchen: I suppose she might be bothered to learn that I'd been watching her—but that doesn't seem likely, with Sharon. She was notably trusting of adults in her classroom—even of a stranger with a video camera. She seemed to experience it as an environment where she could be comfortably in control, taking initiative and expressing herself freely.

Betty: And she's such a skillful player! In this episode she was taking the roles of three or four players simultaneously and playing them out in a script that became more complex as it evolved. She was able to create and then use a whole private world in miniature. Clearly this is an important play opportunity for Sharon, one that her teacher should be sure to make regularly available.

Gretchen: Different adults' values certainly do pop up in their teaching, don't they? I loved Sharon's vigorous defense, to her twin girls, of the importance of going to school: "She gonna go to school! Let's go to school. . . . You gotta stop fooling around in this school!" It would never have occurred to me to correct Sharon's addition facts at that moment, charmed as I was by Sharon's imagery; but Mrs. Turney, the classroom aide who knows these things are important, was prompt and even indignant in her correction: "Two plus two is four!"

Betty: School is more than isolated facts; it's high drama, and Sharon knows that. This was drama Sharon invented, playing alone with miniatures. In the next observation, things are different; she's confronting the real-life drama of being a stranger in a new group. Let's see how she does it.

SECURING A PLAY SPACE

Special arrangements have been made for Sharon to attend the afternoon preschool class this week. She knows the teachers but not the children, most of whom speak Spanish, which Sharon doesn't understand. As the observation begins, Sharon, wearing a floor-length green medical gown and high-heeled red shoes, has joined a conversation between Georgia and a resource teacher.

Pushing a doll buggy, Sharon returns to the housekeeping area, where two girls are holding dolls in their arms. Sharon begins to clown for their benefit. She "slips" down onto the floor, and while lying on her side she kicks her high-heeled feet in a scissors kick. The girls laugh, as does Sharon. She sits up, kicks her red shoes loudly against the floor, and laughs loudly, as if to encourage the others' laughter. Next she takes the shoe off her right foot and bangs it on the floor, enjoying her own merrymaking.

Sharon stands, puts the shoe back on, and walks over to the two cash registers on the shelf. She lifts one high above her head and carries it to the doll buggy. "Put that back!" calls a child. Sharon ignores these words; in another show of defiance, she takes a cup off the shelf. A child warns her, "I'm gonna tell Georgia now." She calls, "Georgia!" Sharon takes the second cash register. "Sharon," calls Georgia. Screeching their indignation, the two girls accompany Sharon as she walks the doll buggy across the room to the table where Georgia is sitting.

"¿Qué pasó?" asks Georgia. Three girls point to Sharon's bags, indicating their objection to the contents. One says, "Sharon take our piggy bank." "Sharon, I don't like that," admonishes Georgia. Sharon turns the buggy around and a bag, containing one of the cash registers, falls out. Georgia calls, "Sharon, Sharon, look, what happened to that bag? Pick it up, pumpkin." Sharon complies, then struts back to the housekeeping area, pushing the buggy ahead of her. She returns one cash register to the shelf, saying in feigned anger to a child, "That's all I have now." She sticks out her tongue and turns on her heel.

Sharon walks past a group of three girls sitting with babies, turns, and says, "I'm not your cousin. I'm not your cousin. Is that your cousin?" There is no response from anyone in the group.

Sharon stomps a heel, puts a hand on her hip, and wheels the doll buggy off. She goes over to the table, where she picks up a plastic dishpan and puts it on her head. On top of that she puts a large square plastic pan. Then she bangs both down onto the table, loudly. Sharon takes some plastic food and puts green beans in a pot, enclosing it with a lid. She builds a sandwich: plastic vegetables between two pieces of plastic bread. She puts both plastic pans, with "food," into the oven.

Sharon then picks up an armload of dress-up clothes from the doll carriage. She lifts them into the round plastic dishpan. She takes a hanger out of one of the gowns. She pretends to wash the clothes in the pan. Georgia calls, "You washing the clothes, lady?" Sharon nods yes. She retrieves the first dishpan from inside the oven and puts some clothes into it. It goes into the oven, followed by a third dishpan filled with clothes. She turns on the "dryer" (oven).

Two of the girls who had complained about her to Georgia join Sharon, exclaiming "¡*Hay ropa!*" as they admire the clothes in the "dryer." Sharon grins. She takes all three tubs out, and sets them across the top of the stove and sink, protecting them with her arms as if someone will steal them. She returns all three pans to the oven. Georgia comes over, asking, "What is that? Why do you put the clothes inside?" Sharon opens the door and begins bringing the pans out.

GEORGIA: Is that a dryer?

Sharon smiles and nods.

GEORGIA: You washing clothes?

SHARON: Yeah.

GEORGIA: Are they ready now?

SHARON: No, not that one.

GEORGIA (*as Sharon turns the knob on the stove*): Not that one? Not that one either? Okay.

A child comments, and Georgia translates: "They say be careful, you'll get burnt." Sharon grins and turns a knob as if adjusting the heat. Georgia says, "The dryer's really hot, isn't it?"

Gretchen: Sharon's play needs today seem quite different from those we've observed earlier, where she was seeking solitude. Today she's actively inviting response from other children.

Betty: That's understandable, since she's trying to make a place for herself in a new group. Partly, she's showing off; partly, I think she's simply trying to establish play space for herself in the face of possible hostility from those whose turf she's just moved into. Her words as well as her actions suggest how she's feeling: "I'm not your cousin, I'm not your cousin." She knows she's an outsider in this group, both because she's new and because she doesn't speak their language.

Gretchen: She did a lot with action rather than words, I noticed—capturing their attention by clomping on the floor with her high-heeled shoes, feigning a fall, and taking the cash registers. That really did make her the star of the show, with attention from her teacher too.

Betty: And it wasn't negative attention. A less sensitive teacher might have overreacted to the "badness"—Sharon's being silly, her taking things, the other girls' screeching, Sharon's sticking her tongue out and dropping things. Georgia stayed calm, just telling Sharon, "I don't like that," and continuing with her usual endearments. (She often calls children "Pumpkin.")

Gretchen: Some teachers might even have said the dishpan doesn't belong in the oven, missing the whole point of Sharon's imaginative play. When Georgia's playfulness coincides with a child's, she's terrifically supportive and appreciative. And the other girls were really impressed.

Betty: As they should be! Both the shopping and the laundry were dramas enacted with imagination and flair. The shopping sequence was long and complex; Sharon has mastered the whole script—dress up, take the shopping cart, put the food in bags, interact with the cash register, insult the neighbors, go home, and prepare a meal. Then wash the dirty clothes and put them in the dryer, while dinner is cooking. This is splendid play, carried on against the odds of living in a hostile neighborhood where your language isn't spoken and you're new on the block.

Gretchen: And Georgia's intervention to ask Sharon about the clothes and the dryer was very helpful, I thought. Her attention to Sharon's clever play ideas served to attract the other girls and name the script for them—a script they certainly would be familiar with and might enjoy playing too.

Betty: "You washing the clothes, lady?" Georgia has herself "seen pattern, given structure" (15), and by calling across the room she alerts the neighbors to washday at Sharon's house. Clearly she was aware that Sharon might need some support, and she offered it within the play script, on which Sharon is the authority. I thought this was a lovely example of a teacher's taking play seriously.

CHAPTER 6

Luanda: Affiliation and Friendship

The video camera has just been turned on, focusing on Luanda. From off camera a child is saying, "I'm not your friend, I'm not Jamica's friend either. 'Cause you don't got a friend 'cause I do got a friend."

Wagging her head, Luanda retorts, "I got a big old friend name Lisa and a big old friend name Aretha."

Gretchen: For me this exchange explains Luanda's passionate interest in sociodramatic play; it's what she enjoys doing most with friends. Nearly every time I visited, Luanda was either playing with other children or busily constructing a setting for play. In three observations, we identified many mutuality-in-social-interaction behaviors (I4) for Luanda.

Betty: Tommy (Chapter 3) was also a very social child, wasn't he? Your observations show him consistently enjoying the company of other children; and he and Dave, his caregiver, played together as well. Was this Luanda's style too?

Gretchen: Unlike Tommy, Luanda did not seek the attention of any of the adults in the room. But she was like Tommy in that much of her activity was embedded in the bubble of dramatic play. Tommy spent a lot of time gathering and constructing the accoutrements he needed for his scripts. Luanda's compelling interest seemed to be in the opportunities for spontaneous social interactions—I detected heightened pleasure in her involvement when there were several other children to play with. Perhaps she enjoyed the complexity and unpredictability that several players bring to cooperative play. The one time I recorded her in a solitary activity—easel painting—she was as involved as ever. But she didn't stay at it for very long; it seemed as though she was taking a break in an otherwise busy morning.

Luanda dips a wide brush into a container of thick pink paint, and securing the paper with her left hand, she makes a bold horizontal line from left to right across the middle of the page. In the bottom half she paints a square, and below it, she places a line of dabs. In the top half she thoughtfully paints a few more lines. Then she pauses to stretch, with both arms and the paintbrush she is holding raised over her head. She takes another minute to fill in an empty space. Then, unclipping the paper, she walks outside to the drying rack.

Betty: That didn't last long, did it? Let's look at one of the observations of her dramatic play, which is much longer.

WATCH THIS SLEEPING BABY

In a somewhat secluded corner near the house area, the teachers had arranged children's books and a child-sized rocker. Luanda has transformed it to suit her play purposes—it is now a living room, a kitchen, or perhaps a front porch. Luanda is attired in a full apron and has a book on her lap. Seated in the rocker, Luanda can watch the doll she has tucked carefully in a doll bed. Jamal approaches.

LUANDA: Hi! you wanna come in? (*Jamal nods and stands beside her.*) My baby's sleeping.

JAMAL (*removing his cape by lifting the tie over his head*): Chokin' me.

LUANDA: Take it off and hang it up. (*She hangs it on a hook for him.*): Goin' somewhere?

Luanda rocks and gazes at the doll. Jamal examines a plastic pair of pliers. Luanda points to one of the hooks, "Unscrew this."

JAMAL (*motioning to go*): I be back.

LUANDA: Okay. Better put your jacket on. Better put your jacket on. It cold out there.

JAMAL (*returning to get the cape*): I'll be back. (*He picks up a book.*)

LUANDA: Could read it when you come back. Better not go to that party's house. That party's house cold in the night. (*She continues rocking and baby watching.*)

Soon Jamal returns. He is wearing the cape and an orange hard hat. Luanda closes her book, looks up, and asks, "You been back, babes? I figure I'll get me ready now. Watch this baby for me."

Luanda walks over to the rack of dress-up clothes. She unties the bow of her apron, lifts it over her head, and hangs it on a hanger. She stands in front of the mirror: "It getting hot out there." "What?" asks Jamal. Luanda repeats, "It getting hot out there."

Luanda is looking through the clothes carefully. Jamal finds a pink straw hat with a bright green ribbon, and places it on her head. He reaches for a cape for himself. Luanda takes a dress off the rack and holds it up in front of her.

LUANDA: You don't got a hat. Put it on.

JAMAL: Okay. (*Luanda places a firefighter's hat on his head. He leans over.*): I dropped my fire hat.

Luanda continues looking through the hats. She hands Jamal a soft furry hat: "Here. Leave your fire hat here." Jamal looks in the mirror to adjust the hat.

ARETHA (*arriving*): Luanda, what are you doing?

LUANDA: Goin' to the party.

ARETHA: Can we get in your house?

LUANDA: Yeah. (*Holding an armload of clothes, she checks on her baby.*): I better watch my baby 'cause she's sleeping.

Luanda chooses a dress from the rack and tries on a hat. She holds up the dress as she calls to Aretha, "Excuse me, can I use this? Excuse me, can I use this?"

ARETHA: Why?

JAMAL: We have to go.

LUANDA (*to Aretha*): Okay. Bye bye. I just going to get me my homework.

Betty: Luanda's so masterly! I love watching her play; she's got the whole complex script and lots of social savvy. The nice use of "excuse me"—what social graces! These children are such fine interactors.

Gretchen: I was fascinated to see that Luanda had appropriated the book corner for her house play.

Betty: Thank goodness, the teachers did not impose one of those irrelevant rules about single-purpose use of space ("Dress-ups stay in the dress-up area; books stay in the quiet area."). If Luanda had been asked to tidy up the book corner and to move to the area designated by adults for dramatic play, the play could easily get shut down. It makes perfect sense that a weary mother needs a good book to relax with while her baby is napping!

Gretchen: Luanda had carried the rocking chair and the doll bed from the house corner and turned the bookcase to achieve a semblance of privacy.

Luanda attends a state-sponsored preschool program for low-income qualifying families that is housed in a big, airy room in a local high school. The program has morning and afternoon sessions, each with an enrollment of 16 children. Six families in the afternoon group speak Spanish in their homes, and one of the two teachers is bilingual. The teachers gradually have acquired some wonderful accessories for dramatic play, including a variety of light- and dark-skinned dolls, doll clothes, clipboards with pencils, a typewriter, all manner of hats and shoes, telephones, and a number of "container toys": plastic and straw baskets and purses, lunch boxes, and small laundry baskets. All of these helped to stimulate complex play.

Betty: One of the ways parents find involvement in this preschool is by repairing equipment and making clothes for dramatic play. The teacher,

Claudia, told me recently that a couple of the mothers who come from Mexico had decided to make a child-sized wedding dress to add to that wonderful collection of dress-up clothes! There's a whole new play script in the making.

Gretchen: When I observe master players, I think of Vygotsky's (El'konin, 1966) idea that dramatic play is the context for beginning players to practice separating actions from objects. The function of an object no longer prescribes how it is used, when the child is pretending. As teachers know all too well, capes typically stimulate superhero play, but these children transformed a cape into a "jacket." Luanda made this clear when she suggested to Jamal, "Better put your jacket on. It cold out there."

Betty: By paying attention to the child's symbols, and trying to name the play script, the adult is helped to appreciate the child's intention in playing (Wien, 1995). It isn't hard to figure out the name of Luanda's script— "Mother cares for the family." Luanda is very masterful in using language to communicate her script to others. For example, she says to Jamal, "Better put your jacket on," or "I better watch my baby 'cause she's sleeping." These are great examples of Luanda's ability to scaffold the play so that a less skilled player can play right along with her.

Gretchen: In expressing nurturance toward a baby and a significant male in the household—perhaps a son or a brother—Luanda was identifying with caring adults. She certainly knew how to play that role!

Betty: And she obviously has a whole head full of possible play scripts.

Gretchen: Yes. One of the reasons Luanda was fun to watch was the unpredictability of her play. To complicate the plot at the end she announces, "I just going to get me my homework."

Betty: She is a young mother with a busy life-style, indeed! Motherhood and school have equal appeal.

Gretchen: Yes. Luanda, who is 4 years old at the beginning of my project, attends preschool in the afternoons. She is an African-American child with big brown eyes, whose hair is always done in neatly braided cornrows with lots of decorative barrettes. Luanda lives at home with her mother and an 8-year-old brother. Her mother too must see the master player in Luanda; she has taken her to try out for television commercials!

Betty: In the first observation, Luanda's co-player was nicely cooperative with her play agenda. Let's take a look at the next one—where Luanda has to do some heavy-duty negotiating to retain leadership of the play.

A WEMON FOR BABY

Luanda and Dulce are at the play dough table together. In the middle of the table there is a plastic tub of homemade play dough and a basket containing child-sized rolling pins, cookie cutters, and golf tees. Luanda is wearing, on top of her overalls, a long pink skirt with blue-sequined straps.

The girls are sitting across the table from each other, each squeezing and pinching lumps of purple play dough. With a laugh, Luanda playfully tosses a rolling pin. It clatters across the table. Dulce giggles. Grinning, Luanda looks at her and tosses a second rolling pin. This one clatters onto the floor. Laughing somewhat self-consciously, Luanda glances up to see if anyone notices. She ignores the camera. Her shoes clap on the linoleum floor as she retrieves the rolling pin.

Luanda sits down in her chair, looks directly at Dulce, and laughs three times in a high-pitched, monosyllabic laugh, "Ha! Ha! Ha!" She pokes a cookie cutter into the play dough and says to Dulce, "Look. I made a wemon. I made a wemon. See? Look what I made, Baby."

Luanda carefully pokes a golf tee into her lump of play dough. Using two hands to hold a rolling pin horizontal, she gently hammers the tee. Aretha, clutching a Cabbage Patch Doll in her left arm, joins Dulce and Luanda. She is holding a clipboard with a pencil attached by a string.

ARETHA: What's your name, Dulce?

DULCE: 794830.

ARETHA (*as she writes*): 7 . . . 9 . . . 2 . . . What is your last name?

DULCE: Dulce Modesti.

ARETHA (*writing and saying*): Dulce Modesti. And what's your last name?

DULCE: Dulce Modestini.

LUANDA (*watching and listening carefully to this exchange*): My name is
     Dulce Cricket.

ARETHA: Dulce Cricket. Dulce Christmas?

LUANDA: Yeh. Dulce Cricket. (*She hammers on a tee and looks beyond Aretha at the camera.*)

ARETHA: What's a boy name?

LUANDA: Wigwa.

ARETHA: Wigwa. I'm the doctor, you guys, okay?

LUANDA: My name is Ca-gu-a.

ARETHA: My name is Dr. Jones.

LUANDA: Hi, Dr. Jones. My last name is Ca-gu-i-coo.

A fourth child, Sally, is at the table now, watching the goings-on. Aretha asks her last name. Sally answers, "Wice." Aretha writes on the clipboard.

Luanda is separating and squeezing her play dough. She looks up at the camera, and as she pulls at the play dough, she smiles broadly with one eye shut, imitating the photographer. Meanwhile, Sally helps herself to one of the lumps of play dough. Luanda quickly reaches to retrieve it.

SALLY (*protesting*): I had that first.

LUANDA: I had it first!

SALLY: I had it first.

LUANDA (*pointing*): No, you didn't, you was over there!

Luanda slaps Sally on her chest, and defiantly squeezes the two lumps of play dough together. Sally does not appear hurt, and she does not attempt to take back the play dough.

Luanda is working with her play dough; she has a golf tee in her right hand and a rolling pin in the left. She begins singing in a clear voice, inventing her own tune: "Happy birthday to Dulce, happy birthday to Dulce."

Luanda looks up at the others and taps the rolling pin in rhythm with her song, "Happy birthday to Dulce! Happy birthday to Dulce . . . Happy birthday. . . . "

The girls are watching and listening. Luanda blows at the upright golf tee, pretending it is a candle. Luanda continues her song, "Happy birthday to Dulce, Happy birthday to Dulce!" Then, looking briefly at the camera, she says, "Got some more pictures!"

Smiling now, Dulce sings the familiar tune: "Happy birthday to you, happy birthday to you . . . "

SALLY (*joining in*): Happy birthday to you . . .

LUANDA (*admonishing Sally*): Her birthday already o'er yet.

Using a more quiet voice, Sally continues singing.

ARETHA (*to Dulce*): Happy birthday!

LUANDA (*singing*): Happy birthday to Chee.

ARETHA (*calling*): I'm Dr. Jones.

LUANDA: I'm Dr. Dick. I'm Dr. Dick.

DULCE: Happy birthday to you, happy birthday to . . .

LUANDA (*joining in*): . . . birthday to Dr. Jones . . . happy birthday to Dr. Jones, happy birthday to Dr. Jones. (*still singing*): Blow the candles out, blow the candles out, blow the candles out!

Betty: At the beginning of this episode, I think Luanda and Dulce were engaged in parallel play with the play dough. That wasn't enough for Luanda, but I found it interesting that in getting Dulce's attention, Luanda didn't use language or focus mutually on the task, as she's certainly capable of doing. Instead she regressed, using a silly (and forbidden) physical action—tossing the rolling pin across the floor—to amuse Dulce and herself. That succeeded in starting a game, and I was waiting to see if a teacher would stop it; I was glad no one did. This was nonmaster play for the sake of initiating mutuality in social interaction.

Gretchen: And how often kids look around in hopes that no one is noticing!

Betty: For a 4-year-old, that's limit testing, not only play. Luanda was also checking to see if you, an unfamiliar person with a camera, were going to behave like a teacher. You didn't, so she was free to ignore you. She went on to use the play dough to initiate master play, using the dough intentionally, and naming it—what did she call it, a "wemon"?

Gretchen: Yes, she called it a "wemon," followed by, "See what I made, Baby." This was her way of saying, "Hey Dulce, let's pretend."

Betty: Wait a minute. I don't get it. She called it a "wemon." Would she say that to a teacher if a teacher asked her to tell what she'd made? Or would she say "lemon"? Can she say *l*?

Gretchen: Of course! Luanda's saying "wemon" because she is pretending to talk baby talk with Dulce.

Betty: Now that's sophisticated play!

Gretchen: Despite what had to be the obvious presence of the camera to these girls, this play felt like very private play to me. No adult came 'round, the way teachers often will, with a teaching agenda ("If you roll the clay this way you can make a snake."), or with the idea that the girls could use a negotiator ("Who will share so that Sally will have clay too?"). I have said that so many times!

Betty: And what good teacher has not? But no adults interrupted these girls, so they got to work on social positioning, which was their agenda. Luanda was making the usual show of leadership about what she wanted to play and with whom, and Aretha literally brought to the table quite a different script. Doctors need patients if they are going to get their names and write prescriptions for them on their clipboards.

Gretchen: And then Sally came on the scene, approaching the play somewhat awkwardly, perhaps. She certainly wanted to be included in the group, and she saw a ball of play dough as her ticket for admission.

Betty: Thank goodness, when Luanda slapped Sally on the chest, a teacher did not feel it was necessary to remind her to "use your words." The girls were defending their turf in a way that was natural to them. It's the way you play in your neighborhood—it's just *not* natural to school. Sally did not appear to be hurt nor did she seem to feel insulted.

Gretchen: So now we have two master players—Luanda and Aretha—in the same space, using similar tactics to involve other players. Aretha succeeded in catching Luanda's interest in her names game.

Betty: What were some of the names she invented? Dulce Cricket . . . Wigwa . . . Ca-gu-i-coo. . . . That's verbal testing and tinkering! Luanda seemed to be practicing language to control and direct the play. The need for power stimulates effective language—you want to grab and hold your audience/co-players, and interesting words do that.

Gretchen: There were several times in this observation that we scored Luanda's verbal exchanges as sees-pattern, gives-structure behavior (I5). The examples in Liz Prescott's Child's Mode of Behavior coding are of sees-pattern structuring with objects. In master play, children also may make their symbols verbally explicit as a way of communicating their meanings to co-players and identifying the rules of play.

Betty: Let's see, wouldn't the way she noticed and incorporated the camera into the script be one of those sees-pattern, gives-structure behaviors? Of course you need a camera at a birthday party! And another one: by singing "Happy birthday, Dr. Jones," Luanda integrated Aretha's competing theme into her birthday party script.

Gretchen: What an ingenious way of retaining control of the script!

Betty: These girls were collectively negotiating for dominance of the script from within the frame of the play. By using the language of both scripts, Luanda both affirmed the caring doctor script and expanded on it: The doctor can come to the birthday party!

Gretchen: As I continue to observe master players in action, I am increasingly appreciative of their ability to negotiate roles and evolve the script from within the frame of the play. These children attend with concentration (I2) indeed! There are no short attention spans here.

Betty: Let's take a look at the third Luanda observation. Here a frustrated Luanda has to come out of her fantasy when another child brings destruction to her play space.

THE HOUSE NEEDS FIXING

Luanda and Laverne are in the block-building area, adding finishing touches to a large, L-shaped block structure. The plastic and large hollow blocks have been stacked as high as their shoulders. Jamie, a high school student who visits the program regularly for her child development class, chats with Luanda, who also is working on the block structure. Luanda basks in the attention of her adolescent friend.

LUANDA (*asking Jamie*): You know our house? Our house is on West Cactus Brook.

JAMIE: West Cactus Avenue?

Luanda nods.

JAMIE: Who do you stay with? Your mommy? Your daddy?

LUANDA: I stay with my mommy and my daddy.

JAMIE: Your brother stay there with you?

LUANDA: Yeah.

LAVERNE: Uh-uh!

LUANDA: Yes he do! I should have brought him over here so I could build
my house. Hi Jamie, look at my house.

JAMIE: That's your house?

LUANDA: Uh-huh.

LAVERNE: You gonna come in our house?

Ricardo takes two small blocks from the structure and carries them
off. Luanda dashes after him, picks up one on the floor and the other from
a shelf. Placing the blocks back in place on the wall, Luanda comments to
Laverne, "We 'sposed to be locking all our doors. We gotta be locking all
our doors. We gotta go . . . 'cause the party is gone. All this stuff is gone."

Luanda begins running a carpet sweeper back and forth along the carpet. Ricardo returns. This time he knocks off two blocks from the wall. Luanda chases him away. Then she restores the blocks, saying "Why you
knock down our beds, stupid? Watch my bed, Laverne. That's your bed in
the middle and that's my bed."

Luanda looks up to see Ricardo and Maria together knocking over the
tallest wall. Luanda pushes Maria, who breaks out in a loud wail.

JAMIE: What happened?

Maria points at Luanda.

JAMIE: What'da do, Luanda?

LUANDA: She knock-ed down my house.

JAMIE: She knocked down your house. (to Maria): Did you knock down
her house? You knocked it down?

Maria gradually quiets down. Laverne has left the area entirely. Blocks
are scattered all over. Luanda halfheartedly rights two blocks. She calls
across the room, "Laverne! Laverne!"

Without looking, Luanda tosses a hollow block behind her across the
floor. Then she randomly tosses several more blocks around the block
area.

JAMIE: Luanda!

LUANDA: I don' want it! I can't fix it!

JAMIE: You can fix it. Just don't throw them.

LUANDA: I need somebody to help me!

Luanda turns her back on the blocks and begins plunking aimlessly at
the keys of a nearby toy cash register.

Betty: I love "locking the doors" as the play-script response when one's
house is invaded. While there, did you have a sense that the sanctity of
Luanda's house needed adult protection from other kids? — or that their

forays were just a fact of life in the neighborhood, and Luanda was competent to deal with them?

Gretchen: I think Luanda handled Ricardo's incursions into her space with good humor, until he and another child completely toppled the structure. That destroyed Luanda's play, and Jamie says Luanda can fix it but she doesn't offer to help—not motivating, and not fair, either! And Luanda got aimless at that point—understandably, I thought.

Betty: I think I would have tried not to let that happen.

Gretchen: It seemed like a missed opportunity for an adult to mediate some shared problem solving by the children.

Betty: I would certainly have offered my help in rebuilding. (All homeowners need earthquake insurance!) I've seen quite a number of teaching staff avoid helping children with any cleanup. I assume their rationale is moral character building; children need to learn to clean up their own messes. It isn't much effort for an adult to clean up, or help clean up; in fact, it's much easier than getting the child to do it. So I can interpret this common behavior only as a moral imperative: If he doesn't learn to clean up at 2 or 3, he never will. There are lots of these moral imperatives in children's lives; adult anxiety about sharing and cooperation, about "just playing," and about success in school seem to be at the root of some of them.

Gretchen: I think that play watching helps teachers to see beyond rules that are sometimes rather arbitrary—no throwing blocks, clean up your own mess—to the underlying reasons for the behavior. Luanda was undoubtedly feeling very frustrated that all her hard work had been destroyed by another child's mischief-making. She called out that she needed some help, and she did; the blocks were in total disarray.

Betty: What's more, with the sudden turn of events, her co-player Laverne disappeared. Luanda probably also felt abandoned by her peers.

Gretchen: My time for filming Luanda had ended, and I turned at that point to observe another child. I did look back, to check on Luanda, and saw that Claudia, her teacher, was sitting with her on the floor in the block-building area, discussing several ideas for rearranging the blocks. But Luanda was only halfheartedly involved; she had run out of energy. My sense was that it might take another child or two to recapture Luanda's interest in the construction. Luanda wasn't a master builder, she was a master dramatist, and the point of building a building was to create a place to play with friends. That was her personal theme as I saw it throughout the observations.

CHAPTER 7

Analyzing Master Play

Our observations and subsequent discussions have confirmed for us that when teachers pay close attention to master players, they learn ways of supporting the play and learning of all children. At this point the reader has "observed" master players in the four case example chapters and hopefully has accompanied us in thinking about the children's play skills as we dialogued. The next step is to "add something new," "examine, test, and tinker," and "see pattern and give structure"—to look more closely at what master play is, through the lens of relevant theories and research on cognitive development, on play and creativity, and on social interactions in play.

PLAY AND COGNITIVE DEVELOPMENT

Piaget described logical thinking as the ability to perform "operations": thought processes that are organized, structured, and reversible and can be generalized. Developmentally, preschool children are not logical thinkers; instead, they know in an intuitive and figurative sense, based on images and perceptions of their immediate experiences. Figurative knowledge, the origin of the child's ability to symbolize, is in Piaget's (1945/1951) view a necessary precursor to logical thought.

> Why is there any need for symbols and make-believe, and not just exercise of conceptual thought? . . . the child's logico-verbal thought is still too inadequate and too vague, while the symbol concretizes and animates everything. But this means that the symbol . . . is the very structure of the child's thought. (pp. 154–155)

According to Piaget, the child invents symbols because she has limited capacity to understand the logical world, and so she distorts reality to her own ego. Pretense begins when the child uses an object in service of the ritual, regardless of its function in real life. In Piaget's view, it is when the child begins to use symbols in meaning making that intelligent thinking is apparent.

Piaget, with his view of the active child as agent in the construction of her own knowledge, contributed significantly to understandings of how children learn. The human mind acquires learning not through the passive reception of facts and information, but in the active pursuit of order and relationships using cognitive processes such as exploration, examination, question asking, discussing, testing, categorizing, recategorizing, sequencing, numbering, and the like. In asserting the child's right to be a "protagonist," the Reggio Emilia schools echo Piaget's vision of the curious, intellectual child (Malaguzzi, 1993).

Similarly, proponents of children's play claim that these same cognitive processes are activated when the child engages in play. Using Piaget's cognitive framework, Smilansky describes a developmental sequence of play sophistication that includes the child's playful ability to construct with materials toward an end (we call these children "master builders") and to spontaneously dramatize real and imagined experiences alone or with others ("master dramatists"). Smilansky argues that children's social pretend play is a cognitively advanced form of behavior: "The complex nature of this type of play is one of its main characteristics" (Smilansky & Shefatya, 1990, p. 28). Well-developed sociodramatic play is cognitively complex because

> it involves not only representation and pretense, but also reality orientation, organizational skills, reasoning and argumentation, social skills, etc. The spontaneous integration of all these elements into sequential and meaningful activity is the essence of sociodramatic play. (pp. 27–28)

A significant contribution by Smilansky has been the development of a play training technique in which teachers guide children in the skills of dramatic and sociodramatic play. Following the training, Smilansky (1990) found, children showed gains in these cognitive-creative activities:

> better verbalization, richer vocabulary, higher language comprehension, higher language level, better problem-solving strategies, more curiosity, better ability to take on the perspective of another, higher intellectual competence, performance of more conservation tasks, more innovation, more imaginativeness, longer attention span, and greater concentration ability. (p. 35)

In Piaget's view, the child's stage of cognitive development defines the limits of the child's abilities. Not so, according to Vygotsky (1933/1978), for whom imaginative play leads the preschool child's development. In his vision of the teaching–learning process, Vygotsky brings together social and cognitive perspectives, suggesting that knowledge is socially constructed. He describes learning as taking place in a person's zone of proximal development, which is "a range of tasks that the child cannot yet handle alone but can accomplish with the help of adults and more skilled peers" (Berk, 1994, p. 30). Through mutual engagement with a more able partner, the child's thinking is "stretched" beyond his or her abilities when alone. Opportunities to operate in one's zone of proximal development facilitate learning, because "the child internalizes the kind of help he receives from others and eventually uses the same means of guidance to direct himself" (McNamee, 1987, p. 290). Social imaginary play, for Vygotsky (1933/ 1978), creates the zone of proximal development for the young child, and "is in itself a major source of development" (p. 102).

Imaginary play is the young child's chance to engage in dialogue and express meanings symbolically; it provides the same benefits as cooperative learning does for slightly older children: "Small groups of peers at varying levels of competence share responsibility and resolve differences of opinion as they work towards a common goal" (Berk, 1994, p. 31). Good play is the young child's growing edge!

Imaginary play is the young child's experimental theatre; it is the arena in which she practices the symbolic communication of ideas. Children's earliest symbols are gestures: An infant waves bye-bye, plays peek-a-boo, and raises her arms to request a pick-me-up. Master players, more skilled in using words and action, conjure invisible objects out of the air. As Dennis (Chapter 4) runs with his arms outstretched in front of him, Peter calls, "I got two pizzas," and Dennis responds, "I got lots of 'em!"

Beginning players typically need objects to imagine with; empty cup in hand, a 2-year-old can fill it with invisible tea and offer a drink to her mommy. Children more skilled in play often ignore the functional attributes of objects, and use gestures and words in combination with objects to bring their own meanings to them. "In play, things lose their determining force. The child sees one thing but acts differently in relation to what he sees" (Vygotsky, 1933/1978, p. 97). Sharon (Chapter 5), who has been "shopping" for plastic food, wheels it off in a doll buggy to the table in the play kitchen. There she puts the food in a pot and a square dishpan and shoves both into the oven. Sharon then picks up an armload of dress-up clothes. She lifts them into the round dishpan that is on the sink and pretends to wash them, using a kneading motion. Her teacher notices and calls, "You washing the clothes, lady?" Sharon nods yes. She retrieves the other dishpan from inside the oven, dumps the food out of it, and puts in clothes. It goes into the oven, and she enacts turning on the "dryer" (oven).

Play frees the child to behave according to the meaning she wants to express, using objects and language in the service of that meaning. Language is a highly significant cognitive achievement because it is the external reconstruction of internalized action, the social expression of personal meaning (Vygotsky, 1934/1962). Language and naming assist the child's representations because the name evokes meaning: A stick can substitute for a horse when the playing child calls it "horse" and animates it accordingly.

From stick to horse is easy; very small children do that. In the Zappers episode (Chapter 3), 4-year-old master player Tommy effortlessly converts a rusty eggbeater into the zapper he needs to defend himself against the enemy observer. Tying it to a rope, he gives orders to his buddy, Mike: "You push this button and I'll . . . " Mike, equally knowledgeable about the rules of this play, obligingly presses the "button."

Tommy turns the handle of the squeaky eggbeater, aiming it at Gretchen; he shoots her with it. "Get her in the eye, Tommy," Mike encourages him, actively participating in the drama. Gretchen chooses to participate, too, playing the same script: "You know what, you missed." The caregiver, however, chooses not to permit the play; this game violates her adult sense of responsibility and rules. "I don't let you hurt people," she says. Note, however, that this response takes the play script seriously; she also is pretending that the eggbeater is a zapper. Only in the play script is anyone being hurt.

Tommy responds to these social constraints; he stops aiming at Gretchen and turns the eggbeater in the direction of the porch. He stops shooting in order to elaborate its function further: "This is a paint blatter that blows people's eyes out." He uses a scoop for its real-life purpose, scooping sand with it; but he pretends the sand is "paint" and pours it on the blatter. Then he aims it at the porch, describing its powers in poetic language:

> You squirt it at your hair,
> your eyes, and
> your mouth.
> Electric paint blatter!

PLAY AND CREATIVITY

"The young child, as a maker of imaginative worlds, is a kind of poet, and is in command of some considerable intellectual resources developed and exercised by such imaginative work" (Egan, 1987, p. 466). Tommy's behavior during this episode has been coded in every variation of the I category, as he uses imaginative language and action to cope effectively with his need for power in the face of the assorted threats to his autonomy that confront him as a child of 4. In his imaginary play, he is creating his own meaning; the child's desire to express meaning dominates over the function, shape, or socially assigned names of objects. In the language of play the meanings of words substitute for the thing; "therefore, in play there occurs the emancipation of the word from the thing" (El'konin, 1966, p. 41).

The research of Dansky and Silverman (1973) is a strong argument for childhood play as a contributor to creative-thinking abilities. Children who had extensive play experiences approached divergent tasks with more flexibility, curiosity, spontaneity, and interest than children who were exposed to imitation or nonplay environments. "Play creates a set, or attitude, to generate associations to a variety of objects whether or not these objects are encountered during play activity" (Pepler, 1982, p. 67).

Dennis is on the edge of the top of the spool. Fearfully he says to Peter, "Yikes, the sharks are gonna get me." As if he is avoiding sharks, Dennis takes a stretching, cautious step from the lower edge of the spool to a large hollow block nearby. With the addition of imagined sharks to the area surrounding a real cable spool and box, Dennis has transformed simple physical activity into compelling drama, sustaining his own interest and inviting a friend's involvement as well. Master players, full of good ideas, are interesting company for their peers and for themselves.

As identified in Pepler's (1982) research, investigative and symbolic play are the two types of play contributing to children's divergent-thinking abilities. Both of these play behaviors are by their very nature open-ended; there are no expectations that children conform to a single way of using the materials or that they complete a task with a prescribed outcome. Looking at materials and loose parts with an eye toward alternative or interesting combinations promotes competence in flexible thinking and comfort with novelty. Representation also develops divergent-thinking abilities, and play watching fascinates because of the creativity of master builders and master dramatists in their use of gestures, labeling, and play with symbols to signify meaning.

Tommy, intending to make a mask "to scare all the teachers and children," holds a large bottle of white glue upside down and begins making gluey lines with it on his paper. Suddenly, he "sees pattern, gives structure" (I5): "Hey, look what I made, Mike! I made a Ninja Turtle!" Adding a dollop of glue to the Turtle's ear, he says, "I made a Ninja Turtle with numchop."

MUTUALITY IN SOCIAL INTERACTION

Dramatic play is the developmental precursor to storytelling. Much like theatre, movies, or sitcoms, 4-year-olds' dramatic play is story-in-action.

The story structure enables children's practice with imaginative uses of language and story. The story-like language of dramatic play supports the child's memory and intention, and we see master players manipulating integrated transformations within the play that sustain, complicate, and evolve a play theme (Roskos, 1990). Roger and Peter think Dennis (Chapter 4) as Donatello is trapped, and Peter asks, "Are you trapped?" "No," answers Dennis. Roger has seen no evidence that Donatello has escaped his rope trap. He says, "Oh, yes, you are." Dennis wiggles his body and swings his arms. Peter asks, "Did you be off?" "Cut. I cut the rope," answers Donatello. The two boys and Donatello dash off.

The scripts that constitute children's dramatic play are a predictable sequence of actions based on children's experiences-in-common (Schank & Abelson, 1977). Scripts are children's representations of the things they know about an event, including stereotypical ideas about people, their roles, actions, objects, and cultural routines. "It is children's participation in specific daily routines and their observation of others in such routines that provide the basis for developing consistent and predictable mental representations of daily life situations or 'scripts'" (McNamee, 1987, pp. 289–290). Scripts organize the play, predicting certain acts and sequences.

Because dramatic play scripts are based on children's experiences-in-common, they are the interesting content around which children's social interactions focus during dramatic play. The most common themes of children's pretend play are cooking and baking, having phone conversations, giving a party, taking mother and baby roles, and becoming superheroes (Goncu, 1993). When the script is a familiar one, even unacquainted children can play together, because their mutual knowledge of an event provides for and supports social interaction.

Scripts are culturally and experientially bound. Sometimes a script that is unfamiliar to a child will preclude her or his involvement in dramatic play. Carlos has used two tiers of large hollow blocks to wall off the block-building area. With an open shoebox tucked under his left arm, and holding a plastic toy trowel in his right hand, Carlos walks along the block shelf rubbing the trowel back and forth along the flat surfaces. Ric enters the block-building area. Inviting Ric into the play, Carlos hands him a second box and toy trowel. Carlos resumes his activity. Ric watches briefly and seems to lose interest, departing in the direction of some lively commotion elsewhere. It wasn't until weeks later in chatting with his teacher that we figured out what Carlos's symbols were: Carlos's father works in construction as a plasterer. Because Carlos knew the script and Ric did not, Ric was unable to play with Carlos in a meaningful way.

Several theorists point out the value of social play in supporting children's ability to construct play symbols collectively (Goncu, 1993; Parten, 1932; Piaget, 1945/1951; Vygotsky, 1933/1978). In our study, Tommy and Luanda were masterful in bringing other children into the script by making their symbols explicit through language. For example, Luanda (Chapter 6) says to her play partner, "Better put your jacket on. It cold out there." We also found that we scored Tommy and Luanda as exhibiting mutuality-in-social-interaction behaviors (I4) more frequently. Another interesting master player in our study (Reynolds, 1992), Jill, often played Land Before Time on the weekends with her 8-year-old brother. At day care Jill's ideas for dramatic play so interested Robert that he was often a willing play partner. Jill, as the child who was knowledgeable about the script, frequently instructed Robert's actions from within the frame of the play; for example, saying, "You have to get down like this because now you lay an egg on the beach."

Goncu (1993) suggests that the development of shared understanding, "intersubjectivity," is supported by opportunities to engage in social dramatic play where, in order to play successfully, children affirm, build on, or extend each other's play ideas. Using play dough and golf tees as cakes and candles, Luanda (Chapter 6) instigates a birthday party script and sings happy birthday to Dulce. Meanwhile Aretha, as Dr. Jones, has been "writing" names and telephone numbers on a clipboard. To include Dr. Jones in the birthday party, Luanda changes the lyrics to, "Happy birthday to Dr. Jones."

Collective symbols in social dramatic play are not necessarily dependent on language. On visiting a friend's preschool program in Pasadena, we found her sitting on the edge of a table observing children's free play. This bilingual teacher, Juanita, was scaffolding the social dramatic play of two 4-year-old girls. They had gathered an array of dress-up clothes in the bathroom, where they would visit every so often to change outfits and shoes. Then they would parade around the room hand in hand. The play had been going on all morning. Juanita told us that one child spoke Spanish, and the other spoke English. Occasionally one child would ask Juanita to translate something she needed the other to know—the rest of the time, language was irrelevant to their shared pleasure in the play.

Learning guides the process of development; the child's social interactions are critical to his skills and processes of thinking. Adults have much to contribute to the development of these skills. Many of Tommy's interactions (Chapter 3) with his caregiver Dave were scored as mutuality-in-social-interaction (I4); they are fine examples of the development of intersubjectivity between a child and an adult. Tommy's reliance on adult ideas in accomplishing his imaginative purposes is shown in this episode.

"Oh, that's what I gotta have. I do have to have that." He walks over and stands in front of Dave, his caregiver. "What do you think I want to have?" he asks. Dave responds, "I don't know, what?" Tommy says, "Remember last night I um, you know . . . "

"Oh, that story I told?" Dave's lively awareness of Tommy's play purposes enables him to intuit what Tommy is remembering—Dave's story about alternative ways to zap bad guys: a feather to tickle, honey to make sticky, a hose to spray. Dave, reinforced by Tommy's appreciation of *his* imagination, is quick to help.

For Vygotsky, the ideal pedagogical relationship between adult and child is a dialogue, in which power is shared between the two. This is the arena in which the child's development is stimulated, in which the role of the adult is "to continually reassess his understanding of the child's competence and make room for the child's new emerging competencies" (Mc-Namee, 1987, p. 295).

DIALOGUE

Master teachers practice their craft by engaging in dialogue with children—and with each other. Here we're playing with ideas, re-exploring our understanding of the I codes.

Gretchen: The I codes define the qualities of good play, don't they? For one thing, good play goes on and on. That's I2—attends with concentration. Watching ongoing play, you code a lot of I2s.

Betty: Yes. And as it goes on, children encounter problems and challenges. They bring their minds to their play, problem solving and staying open to possibilities. Play challenges their thinking. That's what several of the codes define.

I3 Adds something new
I5 Sees pattern, gives structure
I6 Tests, examines

Gretchen: Sociodramatic play is reciprocal, too. It involves a lot of I4—mutuality in social interaction. Master players are good negotiators with other children; they often get their way, but they are able to give in gracefully part of the time.

Betty: I think your data point up another useful skill, as well—one that hasn't ever hit me so clearly before. I1b—copes with social constraints—identifies the skill that enables kids to meet their play needs in ways that are both empowering for themselves and respectful of others—especially adults.

Gretchen: Say more. I'm not quite clear what you're getting at.

Betty. Okay. Do you have a handy example of an I1b in your head?

Gretchen: Yes, indeed—since we've just been talking about Dennis. We scored Dennis the highest of all the children in our sample on I1b. One incident that comes to mind is when Dennis and his friend Peter were playing on a box-and-ladders structure in the yard, and another boy began climbing up the ladder. Dennis said to him: "This is not your house, it's our house." An alert teacher promptly intervened: "This is for everybody. If you want to have a house and hide in it you can take some of the blocks and make your own, okay?" And Dennis agreed, saying to Peter, "Yeah, we can make something with blocks," and they went inside together.

Betty: Why is that I1b? Wasn't Dennis just giving up his good idea and conforming to what the teacher said?

Gretchen: We didn't code it that way. In the observation, it looked like more than compliance on Dennis's part. He accepted the teacher's limits without a fuss, but he also took her good idea and made it his own: "Yeah, we can make something with blocks," he said enthusiastically to Peter, keeping the initiative in their play, asserting his own wishes in his response. That's healthy strategy for coping with authority no matter where you encounter it.

Betty: I especially remember Dennis's reactions to your camera. Did you code those as I1b too—when he decided you were the enemy?

Gretchen: Yes. He couldn't get rid of me, so he incorporated me into his play. I think that's very effective coping. It kept him, as chief pretender, in charge of the action, even though in the real world grownups are in charge.

Betty (suddenly): I1b is the social equivalent of I5 (sees pattern, gives structure), isn't it?

Gretchen: Now it's my turn to need an example. What are you getting at?

Betty: I5 is *invention* of cognitive constraints by the child. Child "responds in ambiguous situation with novel but fitting constraints. . . . Child . . . call[s] attention to pattern which was not formally present" (Prescott et al., 1975, p. 9).

Gretchen: Oh, so he's taking charge again—defining the situation by pretending something about it?

Betty: Yes. I think of I5 as the "aha" experience—"Now I've got it!" It can include defining the problem you have solved, or solving the problem you have defined. It involves naming what's there or inventing a classification scheme. These are discoveries that don't happen in closed tasks, where someone else has defined the problem.

Gretchen: Solving closed tasks is I1a—shows recognition of built-in constraints. It's defined as implying skill in a task that has right and wrong aspects, such as puzzles or matching games.

Betty: Schools are full of opportunities for I1a, but in many classrooms I5 isn't particularly valued and may even be discouraged. Do you remember Shirley Brice Heath's (1983) story in about how children from the low-income community she called Trackton behaved in preschool? At home, children played outside, improvising with whatever materials happened to be lying around, so at school they insisted on taking toys outdoors. Since they were accustomed, at home, to "using toys for purposes they created, not necessarily those which the toy manufacturer had envisioned" (p. 275), they were puzzled by teachers' expectations that toys would be used in designated places for designated purposes. Here's Heath:

> When told to "play," they interpreted play as improvisation and creation, and these called for flexibility in the mingling of materials and the mixing of items from different parts of the room. A truck which had detachable parts and was kept in the puzzle corner was to be taken to the sandbox where water and sand could be mixed, the tires changed, and the spare truck parts hauled. If a particular piece of a puzzle looked like a wrench or a jack for a truck, or a spoon for feeding a doll, Trackton children went to the puzzle shelf to incorporate it in their play. Teachers despaired when they found what they classified as puzzles in the sandbox or the doll corner. They said repeatedly, "Put the puzzle pieces where they belong." "When we finish our puzzles, we put them up (or away)." These directives seemed to have no meaning to Trackton children. (pp. 273–274)

Gretchen: These are children who would have scored very high on I5 but very low on I1a and I1b, recognizing setting and social constraints, aren't they? They must have truly frustrated teachers for whom order—teacher-defined order—was first priority.

Betty: Heath, in her book, goes on to describe some of her work with teachers in which she helped them to understand the environments the children were coming from and the strengths they brought to school. Being able to recognize "sees pattern, gives structure" as a strength might have served as some balance of appreciation of the children who were otherwise driving their teachers up the walls!

WHO SUPPORTS PLAY?

In this book we are focusing on how teachers, by watching children, can learn to support their play. In many societies adults have been too busy working to pay attention to children's play, or have regarded children as inappropriate companions for adults. In most societies, however, children have had easy access to play partners of varying ages within the family or neighborhood. Some of these were older children given responsibility for younger ones and expected to keep them contented. What do you do to keep a small child contented? You play with her—and so more skilled players were always available and motivated.

In this process, the older children got lots of practice in being master players. Research in cultures in which toddlers learn pretend play skills from the older siblings who play with and care for them while mothers are busy with other responsibilities has found significant differences in older children's scaffolding skills in support of play. In an experimental task,

> three-year-old American children experienced more complex play with mothers, and Mexican children engaged in more complex play with their 3½ to 7-year-old siblings. Furthermore, Farver (1993) observed that American siblings tended to rely on intrusive tactics; they more often instructed, directed, and rejected their younger partner's play. In contrast, Mexican siblings used more behaviors that gently facilitated pretense—invitations to join, comments on the younger child's actions, suggestions, and positive affect. In this respect, the Mexican siblings were similar to American mothers in their scaffolding, a skill that appeared to be fostered by the Mexican culture's assignment of caregiving responsibility to older brothers and sisters. (Berk & Winsler, 1995, p. 78)

Some American children also learn such skills in their homes. Others may have opportunities to practice them as members of mixed-age groups in schools or child care centers.

> Older children's abilities are validated by their spontaneous assumption of "teaching" roles with younger children. When an adult who was saying Hi to children in the early morning said "Hi" to Megan, Megan said, "I'm sorry, I can't talk to you right now. I'm teaching Bryan Spanish." She was walking around with a pointer, showing him the words on the walls.
>
> Often I write children's dictated stories, reminding them that they have a lot of good ideas and that I am a very slow writer. If I am busy writing with one child, an older child can gently redirect an impatient younger one by offering to "write" his story for him. When Fernando and Brad couldn't wait, Delfine graciously took up paper and pen, mimicking a "teacher voice" and the questions I was asking to write a hamburger story. She filled a paper with kid writing. The younger children were satisfied that their words had been noted and recorded, Delfine felt good about solving the problems of a tired and about-to-lose-patience teacher, and I was gratified that her problem-solving had been so effective. We hung our writings on the bulletin board (after Delfine had translated her writing for my benefit). (Read, 1992, p. 62)

Contemporary child-rearing arrangements in the United States and some other countries typically separate older and younger children. Not only do preschoolers not have much access to 6- to 8-year-olds, but toddlers and 2s rarely have access to 4s and 5s. Some child care programs, like the site of the story just told, do provide fruitfully for wide-age "family grouping." More typically, the modeling of play skills that happens naturally in multi-age informal groups has been replaced by age-segregated groups in school-like settings where adults determine schedule and "curriculum." Curriculum may or may not have room for play.

Play, however, is both developmentally appropriate and culturally relevant for all young children, including those regarded as at risk for school achievement. Direct teaching and rote learning in early childhood fail to ensure lasting school success, even when they produce temporary test results, because they provide an inadequate base for the higher-order thinking skills that are needed in later schooling and in adult life. These skills have their foundation in play—in initiative taking, problem solving, and innovating within the constraints of reality.

In a society in which young children are segregated in age groups under the direct care of adults called teachers, the primary role—an active role—of these teachers is to scaffold children's learning through play. By paying close attention to the play of children who have mastered play skills, teachers become increasingly skillful in supporting the play of all children. From young master players, adults can re-learn how to play.

CHAPTER 8

Becoming a Play Watcher

How do we know what children are doing and learning? We watch and listen to them, paying attention to the details of their action and language. We interpret what we see and hear; we "see pattern, give structure" to our observations, because this is how human beings make sense while they are playing. In the "pretend" of play, children are "a head taller" than when they're only trying to adjust to the "real world" as defined by adults. Watching their play, we become more knowledgeable about their interests, their feelings, the issues they face, their achievements, and the gaps in their understanding. If we are teachers, parents, or other caregivers, this knowledge enables us to define the child's zone of proximal development—the window of opportunity within which we can help her learn and grow (Vygotsky, 1933/1978).

As play watchers, what do we look for? No observer can look for everything at once, although the challenge, "Write down everything the child says and does for 5 minutes," can be a useful one. Instead, we typically approach play watching with an agenda, some ideas of what we're looking for. How competent a language user is this child? How does he handle aggression by other children? How long is her attention span? Which activities does she choose from day to day?

Observation guidelines may come from learning objectives and assessment tools (e.g., Genishi, 1992; Jones & Meade-Roberts, 1991), from an adult's curiosity or concerns about a child (e.g., Paley, 1984, 1990), and from the need to plan curriculum emergently, in response to children's genuine interests and questions (e.g., Edwards, Gandini, & Forman, 1993; Jones & Nimmo, 1994). One teaching challenge is to pay attention to an "invisible" child in your class—one whom you're never aware of and about whose activities you have no idea (Rabiroff & Prescott, 1978). What *is* she doing, and why is it so easy to ignore her? Another useful challenge is to pay attention to children's use of a particular activity area, as Vivian Paley did in *Boys and Girls: Superheroes in the Doll Corner* (1984). Which children play there, and how do they play? (Berk & Winsler, 1995; Stritzel, 1989). If the play concerns you, could you change it by rearranging the space?

As noted earlier, the Child's Mode of Behavior coding (Prescott et al.,

1975) originally was designed to collect data in a research project on the quality of children's experience in child care. Used systematically by an observer without teaching responsibilities, it provides information that can be sorted and counted. Used casually by a working teacher, as ideas of what to look for and interesting names for behavior, it can generate insights to be reflected on and discussed with colleagues, in the never-ending process of theory building that teaching is.

TEACHERS AS THEORY BUILDERS

Developmental theory is taught more often as something to *learn* than as something to *do*. Anyone who takes responsibility for children, however, interacts with them on the basis of a theory, most often unspoken, about who children should become and how to get them there. "You have to make them mind." "Give 'em lots of love, and they'll grow up loving." "Teach them their colors and numbers, so they'll have a head start in kindergarten." The whole theory, in each instance, is much more complicated than these summings-up, and while most people don't invest a lot of energy in sorting it out, they act on it daily.

Teaching and caregiving and parenting aren't simple mechanical actions that become routine with practice, although many people who do them try to make them so. The objects of their attention are wiggly ingenious child-people with constantly changing agendas of their own, busy building their own theories about what grownups will and won't do for and to them and under what conditions. An educational theory is most likely to be effective if it takes the active child into account and if it is used to shape a process of continuing reflection on practice (Wassermann, 1990), by which a teacher continues to refine her own theory. Theories—including those invented by people who became famous for them—are built on observation, reflection (what's going on here?), hypothesizing (making thoughtful guesses about what's connected to what), predicting and testing, and doing the whole sequence over again. Wassermann calls the process of doing this with children "play, debrief, replay." Good teachers do the same thing. They do it best in dialogue with others—colleagues and mentors—working in their own "zone of proximal development" to become more intentional in their teaching (Jervis, 1996).

INTENTIONALITY

To be intentional is to set conscious goals and do conscious problem solving. Intentionality seems to be dependent on language, on inner or actual speech, which makes possible both planning and reflection on outcomes. The accomplishment of complex tasks is much more effective when it's intentional rather than trial and error. What we call *intelligence* and *creativity*—both highly desirable attributes—are habits of attentiveness and intentionality leading to effective, imaginative problem solving.

The I of the codes we've been playing with in this book stands for *integrative* in its original research formulation. The theories from which the Child Behavior Inventory was developed describe a developmental ordering of behaviors as moving away from (rejecting), moving against (thrusting), or moving toward (responding) (Erikson, 1950; Horney, 1945). As discussed in Chapter 2, behavior that is both responsive and thrusting was defined as *integrating*—a more sophisticated level of action, at which the child pays attention to the context while taking self-directed action (Prescott et al., 1975).

"Why do you have to call it *integrative?*" Gretchen asked Liz Prescott recently. "People don't understand what that means."

"You don't," said Liz, promptly. "That's just the word that made sense at the time. What would you like to call it instead?"

Intentionality had already occurred to us in an earlier discussion, and we tried it on Liz, who liked it. We agreed, too, that integrative, intentional behavior, as seen in play, is the major accomplishment of what Erikson (1950) called the developmental stage of *initiative*. In this stage, the preschool child, having mastered basic language and tackled with some success the challenge of the two preceding stages—*trust* (responding) and *autonomy* (thrusting)—is able to use her sense of safety and the competences she has been practicing as a toddler to initiate deliberate action, to innovate within a system of rules of play, to assert her identity. "I pretend, therefore I am," are Paley's (1988) words to describe the importance of play at this stage. Within "the small world of manageable toys" (Erikson, 1950, p. 221), the child creates herself as an independent person who *can do* (Wassermann, 1990) for herself and, increasingly, with others.

Mastery of play is the most important learning in the early childhood years. Becoming a play watcher is essential for any teacher who wants to know if the children in her care are succeeding, and if she is.

HOW CAN I WATCH PLAY? I'M TOO BUSY TEACHING

What's teaching? Talking to children in a group, is the first picture that comes to mind—giving instructions, giving information, reading stories, singing songs. Teachers of young children also do a lot of general supervision (watching to see that everyone's safe) and intervention when there's trouble—resolving conflicts, soothing hurts both emotional and physical. They help with physical tasks, too—tying shoes, washing hands, buttoning, pouring milk—and they do a lot of housekeeping—putting out materials and clearing them away. Where's time to stand back and just watch?

There are many things young children can't do for themselves, but the more time and patient assistance they're given, the more independent they become. Some 4-year-olds yell, "Teacher!" every time another child does something they don't like; others have, with lots of adult support when they were 2 or 3, become competent negotiators and problem solvers who only occasionally need adult help. In some classrooms, children have to wait for an adult to dole out paper, scissors, or tape; in other classrooms, children have been taught how to get their own supplies as needed. In some classrooms adults are alert to interfere any time a child starts to move dishes from the playhouse into the block area, or to drive a truck all around the room; in other classrooms children are free to combine materials from different areas in support of the emergent logic of their play. The day in some preschools is divided by many frequent transitions from one activity or one space to another; because children can't self-manage such transitions, they keep adults busy and preoccupied. In some other preschool programs, children may determine their own rhythm of activities within a 1- to 2-hour play time uninterrupted by the clock.

Competently playing young children are at their most mature; in play, they are capable of self-direction and responsible, appropriate behavior with minimal adult intervention. It is possible to be a competent play watcher in a program where children's play is taken seriously—where the stage is set in space and time (Jones & Reynolds, 1992) and where children are taught the skills they will need to deal responsibly with materials and with each other.

WHAT SHALL I LOOK FOR?

Many teachers and caregivers aren't in the habit of serious play watching, and if they're challenged to try it, they don't know what to look for.

Gretchen: They could look for developmental stages in play, as some of the early researchers (Parten, 1932) did: solitary, parallel, cooperative. Which children are in which stage?

Betty: But you can't do much with those, unless you think it's your job to try to get parallel players to start cooperating. I think it's more useful to think about observation categories that help people teach—that lead them to see more and to respond appropriately.

Gretchen: Okay, but how about observing what the teacher does, while children are playing: What works, what doesn't work, what you'd do differently next time and why?

Betty: That tackles the question of responding appropriately, certainly. But if you're the teacher-being-play watcher, you can't observe yourself. I suppose you could observe another adult in the class, but she might not like that, unless it was her idea. I thought we were talking about observing children.

Gretchen: You're right, we were. How about identifying the master patterners and master dramatists (Wolf & Gardner, 1979)? Which children choose primarily to construct patterns with materials—blocks, paint, little animals, collage? Which children need a cast of thousands—or at least two—to act out their ideas and have mastered sociodramatic play? Think of the differences we saw between Sharon and Tommy.

Betty: I could happily watch for those differences; I find them fascinating. Pat Carini (1986) has inspired me in her work on how different children organize their experience of the world, and I'm always curious about things like that. But suppose I'm a teacher wanting my observations to be *useful*; what could I do with observations like these?

Gretchen: If I were having parent conferences, I'd certainly bring them up, to validate the child's style of being in the world and let the parent know how much I appreciate it. Sometimes parents (and teachers) have a fixed view of what a child *ought* to be like, and it can be helpful to know, if the child isn't like that, that he has some major strengths nonetheless. He isn't a leader in dramatic play, but he builds extraordinary castles.

Betty: As a teacher, I also find that being aware of differences like these helps me acknowledge them to the child—"You've been building for a long time, and you really figured out how to make those tall blocks stand up, didn't you?" It also enables me to think about more materials or ideas that might continue to expand his play.

Gretchen: Watching dramatic players, I can get really interested in the scripts they're playing—both the name of the script and its sequencing and detail. How well do the children know the script they're playing? Could I help them elaborate it?

Betty: Examples, please.

Gretchen: Okay. It's pretty predictable, in a classroom of young children, that the scripts being played out over a period of several months will include cooking, eating meals, caring for the baby, shopping, telephoning, driving the car, police chasing bad guys, firefighters putting out fires, doctors fixing people—what else?

Betty: How could you forget superheroes, in their various guises? They're all variants of bad guys/good guys conflicts, aren't they? Fierce animals—dinosaurs, lions—often have a bad guy/good guy flavor, too.

Gretchen: And teachers like some scripts better than others. Children don't always behave "a head taller." They like to run, to yell, to be silly, to create dramatic action in order to enliven the maddening slowness and seriousness of a world planned by adults.

Betty: Just like adolescents, I often think—and for the same essential reasons: They're bursting with physical energy, and they're trying to establish their identity in the world.

Gretchen: And the drama of adult disapproval enlivens a humdrum day. This is the "bad play" that Brian Sutton-Smith (1985) likes to write about—the kinds of play kids engage in when they're not being watched closely by adults.

Betty: Both adolescents and young children often fantasize that they're invulnerable. Children trust that grownups will take care of them, and so they take physical risks, pushing the limits. If they succeed, they gain competence—as well as satisfyingly dramatic response to their foolhardiness.

Gretchen: Are you implying that teachers shouldn't stop children's risk taking?

Betty: They can't stop it all, nor should they. They should certainly calculate the risk; direct intervention to stop behavior is frequently the only safe response. But forbidding high-energy play usually only postpones it. Children really do need to deal with issues of strength, speed, and power (Skelding, 1992).

Gretchen: And adults can help them do that by imaginative elaboration of unfocused physical activity, as well as of superhero play (Carlsson-Paige & Levin, 1987; Gronlund, 1992). Remember Dave with Tommy?

Betty: If I'm trying to develop an emergent curriculum, it's helpful to me to keep noticing which scripts children are playing—to make a list, even. And to think about whether I can bring in books about those themes, or some new materials that would add to the play. I might want to observe the play closely to retell it to the children as a story and see where that takes us (Jones & Reynolds, 1992; Torgerson, 1994).

Gretchen: If I'm interested in the quality and quantity of children's language, their play scripts are a great place to listen for that, and write down as much of it as I can. Children talk more and better while they're playing than at any other time. Certainly better than when a teacher is asking them questions in a group, even though some programs define that sort of activity as "language development." When I've observed such groups, the teacher was usually doing most of the talking.

Betty: A teacher interested in particular children's social skills might be able to do some identifying of how they use language—its functions during their play. Is this child good at "using her words," and for what purposes? Does she contribute good ideas that entice other children to play with her?

Does she insist on being in charge, or is she good at give-and-take? Is he aware of other children's feelings, and sympathetic to them? Does he do a lot of teasing and name-calling, and if so, what's his purpose — is he trying to get into the play but doesn't know how?

Gretchen: Observing play always begins with the child's agenda, doesn't it? What is the child's purpose? Is she practicing a task grownups do? Asserting power? Creating aesthetically pleasing patterns? Sustaining a friendship? Playing out fears or anxieties? Play serves many purposes for children.

Betty: And if we want to support their growth in intentionality, we should avoid interrupting play as much as possible. Instead we should try to keep learning, both about the children and about our own teaching, by watching them.

CHAPTER 9

Becoming a Master Teacher

A master teacher is a skilled play watcher who not only can observe objectively but can make informed inferences about the play — what it's about, where it's heading — and choose, from a repertoire of possible responses, which to use at a particular time. A play-focused curriculum does not imply a less active teacher than a teacher-directed curriculum, but she is active in quite different ways; her behavior is integrative and intentional, just as the children's is. Playing "teacher" in the conventional sense nearly always undermines play.

A simple arrangement of eight chairs in double rows in the corner of the 3-year-old room has been stimulating bus play for several days. Today several boys have donned Batman capes. "I blue Batman, they orange Batmen," explains one. They are roaming the room, as are several girls in high heels. "Okay, Batman," says the teacher assistant. "What's Batman going to do today?" "Drive the bus," says one of the orange Batmen. They board the bus. A little later, as the assistant walks by, she observes: "Oh, you're driving the bus. Where's the bus going today?" "To school," the driver decides.

The lead teacher has put on a record and is clapping and dancing. She grabs the hands of a couple of girls as they high-heel by, and they dance with her. She organizes a parade with instruments.

Play flows around the room. From time to time there are half a dozen bus riders, some with babies. Orange Batman is heard asking, across the room, "Want to go with us on the bus?" Blue Batman: "I'm reading a book." "I leaving! I leaving!" calls the bus driver.

Lead teacher: "Okay. Five more minutes to clean-up; we're going outside and paint. Let's take off your Superman cape," she says to Batman. "Children who are very quiet can help carry the paint out."

The children, who have been playing for only half an hour, have shown no sign of readiness for a new activity. But the teacher, who loves to paint and has decorated the room with her creations, is happiest when she can be the star, and now she is eager for them to play *her* good idea. In contrast, her assistant, who has no wish to be the center of attention, has been quietly extending *children's* good ideas. (Jones, 1993b, p. 30)

The lead teacher, because she got bored, or because *parade* was on her lesson plan, arbitrarily introduced her parade without response to the children's activity. Intervening in Batman, she called it Superman; clearly, she wasn't paying attention. The children's agenda was ignored altogether; there was no hope that this teacher would take their life seriously; rather, she was superimposing her own. Children's experience at school is often like that.

TO INTERVENE OR NOT TO INTERVENE?

Except for the imminence of the next transition in the schedule or for authentic threats to safety, the only reason for an adult to intervene in children's play is to sustain or enrich the play. Play that is in danger of breaking down through conflict or failure of good ideas needs an adult to mediate conflict resolution or to add a prop or an idea. Skilled intervention takes place within the script; it matches the name of the play.

During the morning a large hollow block structure, first built by two children as a house, has become a park bench, a bus, and now a train, with five passengers and a boy in the driver's seat. "You ready?" he asks the group. Marvin runs up with a doll and an elephant and hands them to one of the girls: "Here your baby. Here your two babies." He climbs on the train, then leaps off it "into the water."

The train starts off "to Chucky Cheese's." It stops as the driver and a passenger purposefully rebuild it, making it longer and lower as they talk about its destination. Karim teeters on a block, then jumps off it. Then he and two other children walk along it, balancing. There are now 10 children on and around the train. Marvin runs off, runs back, and tentatively tips the highest block.

The teacher, Alma, joins the ride, putting an arm around Marvin. "Where are we going?" she asks. "We going to Chucky Cheese!" say both Marvin and the driver. "What are we going to eat when we get there?" asks Alma. "Pizza!"

"We're here!" Marvin announces, and they all get off. "Where are we going to eat our pizza?" asks Alma, as she and two girls move toward the playhouse. Everyone else gets back on the train. "We're leaving!" "Stop for me on the way back," calls Alma, as she begins to sort doll clothes. "What you doing?" asks one of the girls. "I'm the mom. I'm picking up the mess," Alma explains.

A collection of small animals has inspired the creation of an animal store. "Mrs. Duke, come see our store," says one of the boys.

MRS. DUKE: Is it safe for me to come in? Do I have to knock?

BOYS: We got a snake! (*They roar at her.*)

MRS. DUKE: I thought they were nice snakes.

DARRELL: These are the little snakes. This is the mama. This is the daddy. They're nice.

SAM (*reassuringly*): They don't bite.

MRS. DUKE: Okay, then it's safe for me to come in.

   Mrs. Duke soon leaves to help another child, and several other children come to the store.

SAM: Mrs. Duke said no one can come in here.

PATRICE (*moving in anyway*): But I'm the doctor.

SAM: No, no one can come in. This is the animal store. We live here.

DARRELL (*pointing a "gun" made of unifix cubes*): We police.

SAM: There's too much girls in here.

   "No guns, Darrell," says Mrs. Duke. "We need to keep it safe for the animals." She negotiates the girls into the adjacent block area, which has its own supply of animals. "We're playing zoo again," Patrice announces. Mrs. Duke sits down at a table to create some green paper money, in case the zookeepers should need to buy more animals from the animal store. "Can I do that?" Sherrie asks.

Relatively unskilled players may benefit from frequent interventions simply to keep the play going, to sustain their practice of the skills a master player needs — which include negotiation, using language for effective communication, elaborating a script, using tools (markers, scissors, paint brushes, blocks), and generating solutions to problems. Skilled players are ready to benefit from cognitive challenges that, while remaining within the frame of the play, stretch their perceptual and logical capacities and demand their concentration.

INTERVENTION STRATEGIES

Challenges of this sort often take place after a particular play episode is over and it's the adult's turn — at a group discussion, for example — to set the agenda.

   "Where did you all go on the train?" Alma asks the group at circle time. "You didn't stop for me on the way back."

   "What train?" asks Janella, who has spent her play time painting rainbows and is now snuggled next to Alma on the rug. "I didn't see no train."

   "Did anyone see a train this morning?" Alma asks.

"Yeah!" "Yeah, me!" "We went to Chucky Cheese!" come instant responses from many children.

"Who went on the train?" asks Alma. "Shall we make a list?" She
prints TRAIN at the top of a large sheet of paper and lists children's names
as they call them out.

Janella wiggles against her, then pulls at her hand. "Yes, Janella?"

"I didn't go on the train," Janella whispers.

"I know," Alma smiles. "You were too busy. What were you busy
doing?"

"Rainbows," says Janella.

"RAINBOWS," repeats Alma, writing it next to TRAIN and listing Janella's
name. "What else was happening around here this morning?"

The list quickly gets too complex to manage, so Alma exercises her
teacher-power. "I'm going to stop writing now, and I'm going to tell a
story. Once upon a time—not so long ago—maybe today, even—there
were some busy people going places and doing things. . . . " And she
weaves together the story of the morning, with lots of help from the children. When Chucky Cheese is again named, she is playfully indignant,
"You never got to Chucky Cheese! Brianna and Cory and I waited and
waited there for you, and you never came back."

As the story is told, this teacher is collecting ideas for extending play.
What do the children know about trains, stations, tickets, pizza parlors,
rainbows, written words, and the other events of the morning? How, beyond the oral and written language she's been using, could she represent
their experience back to them? In which of the "hundred languages of
children" (Edwards, Gandini, & Forman, 1993) could they further represent it for themselves? The questions and possibilities are endless, and if
they spark both children's and adults' interest, investigations may continue
for a long time (Jones & Nimmo, 1994).

To investigate an idea in depth, both children and teachers need time
for reflection. Children struggling to understand the world and an adult
struggling to understand children's thinking both need incubation time for
their questions. Genuine questions asked by a curious play watcher, even a
day or a week or a month after the play happened, may be the best of all
teaching tools in focusing thoughtful attention on important ideas.

Vivian Paley (1986), who has learned to ask questions in order to "listen
for the answers I could not myself invent" (p. 125), has written of her
discoveries about children's understanding of human relationships. Here's
a story of her curiosity-motivated intervention in a conflict between two
children.

William has been invading Marni's house play, and their teacher, who has just decided to give up the time-out chair, has thereby forced herself "to observe the way children think." Marni proves willing to examine the logic of his behavior as the "angry wolf" he claims to be. She says she'll be his mother wolf.

"No mother wolf! A angry wolf don't gots a mother. G-r-r-r-r!"

"Teacher, William's doing it again! He's being bad."

Perhaps so, but I no longer had to decide if William's behavior was punishable. Instead, I was listening to the plot . . . I was able to ask:

"Why can't an angry wolf have a mother?"

"Mothers aren't in the forest. They're in the den," he answered soberly.

"When you're in the den you're not angry?"

"Only in the forest is where I'm angry."

"And not in houses," Marni adds. "I'm a different mother in a house."

"Could a different mother in a house give food to an angry wolf?" I asked.

"If he doesn't growl," she replied. (Paley, 1990, pp. 89–90)

Another strategy for teachers is to scribe children's words and/or retell stories of their play (Jones & Reynolds, 1992). "'Once upon a time,' said Joan to her small class of 3-year-olds . . . as their 'going camping' play was coming to an end . . . 'there were one, two, three, four, five, six, seven, eight children who went camping together'" (p. 125).

Linda Torgerson (1994) has written about the power of shared stories to build community while enriching play.

Last week many children were wearing our little piggy hats and tails around the play yard. These were sewn by a parent years ago and donated for the children to play with along with several wolf hats and tails. . . . Tanya and Holly crawled into the empty wooden bike house with several others who were wearing pig accessories. I approached the house, knocked and said, "Little pigs, little pigs, let me come in!" Tanya squealed, "Not by the hair of my chinny chin chin." Then I huffed and I puffed and tried, with the help of many bystanders, to blow that house in. "Is this house made of bricks?" I asked. "Yes!" they shouted from inside. (p. 16)

INTERVENING TO CHANGE PLAY

Some interventions take place in order to change play the adult doesn't like into play she or he can approve of. "No guns, Darrell," said Mrs. Duke. "We need to keep it safe for the animals." Dave (in Chapter 3) ruled against shooting games but offered creative alternatives to capture children's interest and model divergent thinking. Gretchen has told elsewhere the story of her intervention into Rambo play defined mostly by running in and out of the doors of the room; as the teacher, she stopped the players to insist that they make a plan for their play.

> Geoffrey called it "Flight of the Rambos." . . . To help them develop the context for this theme, I urged that we decide on a few rules for their play. The cardboard tubes they had were to be telescopes. And they wanted to build flying ships for themselves out of large hollow blocks. I asked several other questions, to help develop their thinking. What is the design for the flying ships? Will you need supplies for them? Who will play the navigator, and who will be the copilots?
>
> Two of the boys wandered away; I think my intrusion had diffused their enthusiasm. But . . . the 4-year-olds collaborated in the construction of one large flying ship. When completed, it had five chairs atop a long row of connected blocks, with five pairs of wings . . . they became involved in deciding what roles each would play, and what equipment they needed. One of them got lengths of plastic tubing from the water table, which they tied around their waists and pretended were oxygen tubes.
>
> They were totally engrossed in this play . . . , behaving a "head taller" than they were normally capable of . . . after my initial assertion for a theme and some rules, the boys took over. . . . Within the limits they had mutually agreed upon, they were free agents of their own actions. (Reynolds, 1988, pp. 88–89)

Betty: Would you have coded those children's running behavior as T (initiating action, or simple physical activity) or as I (attends with concentration)?

Gretchen: I thought it was T. I wanted to move them to I.

Betty: Aren't you rationalizing, being an adult who refuses to acknowledge the children's invention (because teachers don't like running)? You chose to name the activity "Aimless Running." But wouldn't they have told you it was "Rambo Is Trying to Catch the Enemy"?

Gretchen: No, I don't think so. I see what you're trying to get at, but I think there's a fine difference.

Betty: Oh?

Gretchen: These boys were thrusting. Their play did not yet have a name because they were not involved in it. The play was closer to simple physical play, and I might code it playful aggressive intrusion—T4. Kids often do this kind of play when they first arrive at child care as a way of looking for something to do. When I team taught in cooperative preschool, we used to say that it took some children a good 15 minutes after they first arrived in the morning to find involving play.

Betty: Well then, probably what was effective about your intervention was that you gave the boys an idea for what their running-and-chasing play might become.

Gretchen: I also named their play, which was like a glue that helped them focus on the same idea for play.

Betty: But you didn't invent the name "Flight of the Rambos." They did.

Gretchen: You're right, those were Geoffrey's words, not mine. But he was responding to my insistence that they make a plan for their play. I don't know if he had the idea before the running or as a result of it.

Betty: That's one of the characteristics of young children's playful planning, isn't it? They plan by acting, not by talking about what they're going to do.

Gretchen: Yes. And I have a question for you. You know your story at the beginning of this chapter, about the assistant who was quietly encouraging bus play and the teacher who started a parade? You criticized the teacher as interrupting play—but didn't you describe the girls she involved as just "roaming the room," along with the Batmen?

Betty: That *is* a good question. Often it's a question of feel—is the adult genuinely respectful of children's intent, or is she taking over with *her* ideas? Children's response is the best clue, and in this case the girls did join the teacher quite happily, so maybe they weren't invested in their play. Certainly I, who have watched this teacher before and pegged her as a take-over type (children's art projects always look remarkably like *her* work, when she's been there), was disposed to prejudge her. Later, when she simply interrupted the bus play in order to start another activity (and called Batman, Superman, to boot!), I don't think there was any question about her disinterest in children's good ideas.

Gretchen: She put on the record and started clapping and dancing before any children were involved, didn't she? Why, I wonder?

Betty: It seemed to me that she just felt like it. As I mentioned, I've often seen her as wanting to be the center of attention. I think she gets bored when she isn't, and so she starts dramatic activities to get children to play with her on her terms.

Gretchen: But she's the teacher, the person in charge. I don't think you're giving her credit for having lesson plans and carrying them out; as you said earlier, maybe "parade" was on her lesson plan for the day, and that's why she introduced it. Many teachers would see that as responsible behavior; you don't let go of your plans just because the children are playing something else.

Betty: Oh dear. That really is a value judgment on my part, isn't it? I saw the assistant as being more appropriate than the teacher was, because she was attending thoughtfully to the children's play ideas. But another observer, or the teacher herself, might not have seen it that way at all.

Gretchen (pushing her advantage): Certainly not. It's okay for an untrained assistant to go with children's flow because she's not responsible for planning. She isn't expected to do serious lessons, just to watch the kids.

Betty: I thought she was watching them very skillfully. She intervened with roaming children by asking, "What's Batman going to do today?" "Drive the bus," said one, and so she focused her attention, and theirs, on the bus script, having acknowledged their announced Batman play. In contrast, the teacher didn't ask; she just took over.

Gretchen: And we both define the assistant's behavior as better teaching—except when I'm playing devil's advocate. Why?

Betty: Because we're observing within the context of the theory we've spent this whole book talking about: Play is the most important thing children do. Good teaching is responsive to it, rather than interruptive of it.

Teachers and parents are always at risk of naming the activity from their own perspective rather than from the child's. That is, of course, how the world works: Adults are in charge, and they get to make the rules. While children are playing, they make the rules; and because play is their most fruitful learning activity, we need to honor their rules if we join them in play, enabling them to keep the power for this little space of time. If what we're doing is refusing to join them in it—telling them to stop it because we don't like it—then we should be honest with them and with ourselves. Much of the time, however, it is in their interest and ours to honor their play.

CHAPTER 10

Analyzing the Integrative Behavior of Master Teachers

It is through play that people of any age generate new ideas; creativity and invention are playful processes. Writing this book, and reflecting on our experience with coding children's play, we had the "aha!" that a code might be used fruitfully to analyze teachers' behavior in response to play, as well. We get to make our own rules for developing this code, as any inventor does; however, we invite readers to reflect on their own experiences and values and to argue with us if they choose.

For our purposes, we have chosen to name the teacher's activity *in the context of the children's play*, and to code only for I behaviors. Since children's master play is defined by its large proportion of integrative behaviors, it seems logical to assume that teachers' effective support of play also will have a large integrative component. Because play is the child's, the teacher's behavior is coded as I only if it is effectively responsive to the play. If the name of the teacher's activity is at odds with the name of the children's play activity, it doesn't integrate, it interrupts. In essence, the coding takes the child's perspective.

CODING TEACHER INTEGRATIVE BEHAVIOR

Within this definition, here is our code, with examples of teacher integrative behavior. Note that none of these behaviors are preplanned; the codes describe teacher behaviors that are spontaneous and responsive to the circumstances of the child's play.

I1a   Shows Recognition of Built-in Constraints; Problem Solves

Focused interaction with a child on a task or with materials presents a cognitive challenge *for the teacher*. In her problem solving, she also is modeling for the child.

- Child is having some difficulty with a large floor puzzle. Teacher sits down on the floor to help; it isn't obvious to her where the pieces go, and she works at it parallel to, or cooperatively with, the child.
- Child is trying to get a bike out of the storage shed and asks for the teacher's help. The wheels of several bikes become entangled, and the teacher puzzles over how to disentangle them, talking about the problem as she works at it and as the child watches.
- Spanish-speaking child, inviting the English-speaking teacher to join in her house play, gives directions in rapid Spanish. The teacher, in halting Spanish, asks her to repeat them.

I1b   Copes Effectively With Social Constraints

When a *child's* behavior is coded I1b, he is coping with social constraints as defined by adults. When an *adult's* behavior is coded I1b, she is responding to the social constraints provided by the rules of the children's play and their wish to continue it. The outcome is a win–win solution in which both the adult's wishes and the children's wishes are satisfied.

- Tommy and the trappers want to build their beds in the middle of the floor and turn off the lights in the room. Joan successfully redirects them to a smaller room where they can do just what they want to do.
- Tommy and the trappers want to kill the bad guys. Dave helps them invent ways to trap the bad guys without killing them.
- Rambo and his buddies are running in and out of the room and around the yard. Gretchen corrals them and asks them to make a plan for their play, which they do. The play becomes more focused, complex, and interesting for everyone.
- Barbara wants the children to help at cleanup time. "You're strong," she says to Batman. "I bet you can carry *two* of these big blocks." And he does.
- It's cleanup time in the housekeeping area. "Since you've finished dinner, it's time to clear the table," says the teacher, standing by the dish cupboard. "I see four plates on the table, and four cups. Can you bring them over here to put on the shelf?" Her idea extends the play while completing the cleanup task.

I2   Attends With Concentration

The teacher's attention is focused on continuing play in which she is a participant or an absorbed observer. An adult responsible for a group of children is unlikely to attend with concentration, for very long, to play in which she is an active participant, unless she is an unskilled newcomer to the field who hasn't yet learned to scan the room frequently. It is usually more appropriate for an adult to move in with a new idea or a brief mutual interaction, to enrich and acknowledge the play, and then move out of it again. However, in a classroom with more than one adult present, it can be both possible and desirable for adults to divide responsibility, with one agreeing to scan the group as a whole in order to free another to concentrate, as participant or observer, on a particular activity.

- Adult and child continue to add pieces to the puzzle until it is completed.
- Adult takes turns with child in playing a Concentration game.
- Adult takes notes as she watches the children's play.

13   Adds Something New

The teacher offers a new prop or suggests a new idea to extend the children's play, and the children respond positively. The addition must fit the play, as defined by the children.

- Child says to teacher, "I'm cooking spinach. Want some?" The teacher responds, "Thank you, but I don't like spinach. Do you have any broccoli? I love broccoli with mushrooms." The child comes over with a plate, "Here's your broccoli."
- Two children are beginning to squabble in the playhouse. The teacher knocks on an invisible door. "May I come in? I've come to tea." The squabble stops, and they serve her graciously. "Is this Earl Grey tea?" she asks, sipping it. "No, it's soap tea," says one of the boys.
- A group of children are building a hospital with large blocks, and playing with medical equipment to treat patients. The teacher puts a collection of signs, and tools for writing signs, on the adjacent table. Children quickly notice them and begin writing signs and taping them on the hospital.

14a   Mutuality in Social Interaction; Reciprocity

The teacher responds to social overtures by a child, on the child's terms (without adding anything new).

- Child says to teacher, "I'm cooking spinach. Want some?" The teacher replies, "Yes, thank you. I like spinach. Mmm." She eats it.
- Two children run out of the room wearing fire hats. As they leap onto bikes, the first child asks, "Mrs. Ding, did you see the fire?" "It's over

there!" she replies. When the second child then says, "Bye, Mrs. Ding," she responds, "Bye, Lester."

- Two policemen on scooters are driving together down the bike path / highway. Collecting leaves for tickets, they repeatedly ticket their teacher, who finally protests, "I don't want any more tickets, I'm good!"
- Four children are making birthday cake, spreading sand carefully into pans. The first child says to the teacher, "It's your turn!" The teacher agrees, "Okay, it's my turn to blow out the candles." When the second child asks the teacher, "More cake?" the teacher responds, "Okay, vanilla. No more chocolate."

14b   Offers Help, Sympathy

The teacher responds to a child's request for help or sympathy, engaging in mutual interaction about a problem. Because adults often provide help and sympathy for children, it is the mutuality of the problem solving that earns this adult behavior an I coding. An adult who scoops up the child and coos, "Oh, you poor baby. Let me kiss it," is providing nurturance in a dependent rather than a mutual mode.

- Child whimpers, "I fell down. See?" showing her knee. The teacher responds, "Ouch. I bet that hurt. Would you like some ice for it?"

14c   Reciprocal Hostile Interaction

Children coded for this behavior typically are *playing* at fighting, engaging in taunting or teasing as a mutually acceptable game, in which each participant's ability to stay cool is being tested. ("The dozens" as played by young African-American males is a prototype of such games. Heath, 1983, describes the socialization of boys as young as 2 into this sort of game, by older males in a Black working-class community.) Within a safe and caring relationship (more often in families than in group care), adults and children sometimes engage in similar behavior, often as a way to defuse real anger or frustration.

- Child, approaching from the rear, tries to tickle a seated adult and succeeds only in poking her. The adult, startled, makes a grab for the child, then laughs and tickles him. The child squirms, shrieks, and tries to tickle back.

15   Sees Patterns, Gives Structure

The teacher may acknowledge a pattern a child has discovered, putting into words what the child has done but not named; or may discover a pattern herself and point it out to the child, receiving positive response from the child.

- Sharon, inventing play in an unfamiliar group where the other children speak Spanish and she is able to communicate only through mime, takes clothes out of the washtub in which she has been pretending to wash them and stuffs them into the oven of the play kitchen. Her teacher, Georgia, gets the picture and asks, "Oh, are you turning on the dryer?" Sharon grins. The teacher turns to several girls watching this drama and explains, "*Mira, ella seca la ropa.*"
- Following an evening potluck, a juice cooler has been left on a table in the children's yard. A child tinkers with its faucet, and the teacher recognizes a new play possibility. "Shall we take that over to the big table so other kids can use it too?" she asks. "Maybe we can get some cups and put some water in it." Eagerly, the child helps carry the cooler to the table.

I6   Testing, Tinkering, Examining

With open-ended materials, the teacher engages in exploration parallel with children. (With closed materials, this usually will be I1a.)

- There is new clay on the art table, and children are beginning to poke and pound and roll. The teacher joins them, exploring, rolling, and shaping to see what she can do with it—both modeling for children and enjoying her own exploration.

We see this coding scheme as a possible tool for defining a broad range of behaviors as *real teaching*, directly supporting children's cognitive and social learning. Master play, as we have described it in children, may include all the I behaviors as evidence of children's significant acquisition of knowledge-in-action. It's an altogether different measure than time-on-task, where the task is prescribed by the teacher or the curriculum.

Similarly, master teaching of young children is much more than the writing of lesson plans and the management of an attentive group during the lesson. In their *behavior while teaching*, excellent teachers encounter cognitive and social challenges (I1a, I1b), engage in play with children and are attentive observers of children's play (I2), add new ideas congruent with the play (I3), engage in mutual social interaction with children (I4), function metacognitively, seeing and naming patterns (I5), and thoughtfully explore interesting materials along with children (I6). Doing all these things, they *model learning behaviors* for children as well as offering ideas and information in a direct-teaching mode. Absorbed in living together, both adults and children keep on learning.

USING THE CODE

Here we list the instructions for using the Teacher Behavior Code, followed by episodes of play and teacher–child interactions in which we demonstrate the coding. Even now we sometimes argue about the best code for some behaviors.

1. Choose a play activity to observe, one in which the adult is involved in some way (watching, conversing with children, adding materials, playing).
2. Name the activity, from the child's point of view (see Appendix).
3. Write a running description of the adult's behavior and words. (If you put each action on a new line, it will be easier to code later.) Include as much child behavior and as many words as you need to provide the context for the adult's behavior.
4. Try coding your observation, using the definitions of teacher integrative behavior.
5. Discuss your codings with an interested friend. Explore your disagreements; what questions do they raise for you? What are you learning in the process?

Episode: Building with Blocks

SERAFINA (*to teacher*): Do you want to play with us?
    We making a choo choo train.
TEACHER: That's a nice train. Where's it going?   I3
    A boy tips over the girls' blocks.
    They run for the teacher.
    She helps them rebuild the train and find places on it
for two boys.   I4b
MAGGIE (*bumped by a falling block*): Ow!
TEACHER: If they fall, you get hurt. Look. Look. (*She points out the
    tippy block and shows Maggie how to straighten it.*)   I5
    Building continues and a splendid tall structure is created.
    The teacher builds along with the children.   I2
TEACHER: Now, Paolo, what happens if something falls
    down? (*She helps him remove the highest block.*)   I5
    Maggie climbs into the block cart, which is now empty,
and Serafina starts to follow her. The teacher asks them to get out.   R3
MAGGIE: I'm taking a bath.
TEACHER: Then build a bathtub. (*She helps organize bathtub building.*

Soon half a dozen children are involved, and two tubs are
     constructed.)   I2
MAGGIE (*to Joellen*): No, get out of my bathtub.
TEACHER: There are two bathtubs. Joellen, say, "Can I take a bath
     with you?" Ask Andrew.   I1b
     Joellen, Andrew said you could, and Maggie said, "No."   I5

Episode: Driving Cars on the Road

It's been a quiet morning, and now children's bodies are telling them it's time to MOVE. Suddenly, it seems, there are a half a
dozen boys driving trains and cars rapidly around and around on
the rug. The teacher calls to them, "Know what? I see my boys going very fast there on the rug, and I don't want them to have an accident. Be careful of each other's work."   I5

She joins them on the rug, adding a calming presence and explicit advice, "Don't bump Alberto's work."   I2

But the boys don't seem able to slow down. At such transition
points in the day, adults can choose either to provide a change of
scene or to move themselves into active roles as stage manager or
player. The teacher assistant heads off Desiree and Raul, "You don't
drive cars inside the house. You park cars in the garage, okay?"   I1b

She helps them organize their driving by bringing a roll of
masking tape to the rug and laying it out in a long curving road.   I3

Delightedly, they drive right along behind her. When a crash
seems imminent she responds by drawing arrows on the road to
clarify which way to go.   I5

Several girls who have been dressing up in the house area, getting ready for a party and then dancing in high heels on the rug,
have come home from their party; they sit down on the road while
waiting for the teacher to help tie their shoes. The assistant, antici-
pating an accident when the cars return, warns them, "You're sitting on the road!" They scramble out of danger.   I5

"Is that a racing track?" the assistant asks the drivers.   I5
The teacher is helping several of the drivers to build a gas station.   I3
"They were out of gas," she explains to the assistant.   I5

"I ran out of gas," Raul announces, pulling up to the station. He
gets filled up and races off.

Teacher announces, "Gary has his gas, he's gone. Kurt has his
gas, he's gone."   I5

The play itself has a clear rhythm—vroom down the road, around the curve, avoid that other car, down the home stretch, and pull up at the station: "My car out of gas!" This time, "Gas station's closed," its young proprietor announces.

Episode: Messing with Wet and Dry Stuff

Outdoors, there's a water table full of suds and another table full of sand. The teacher assistant is drawing faces and writing children's names on balloons, which they take to play with. Rory playfully blips his teacher with a balloon and calls her "Mommy."

TEACHER: "I'm not your mommy, and you got me all wet."	I4c
RORY: You ain't wet.	
TEACHER (*showing him*): You got me, right there!	I4c
JASMINE (*at the sand table*): I'm making a cake.	
TEACHER: Did you get to lick the bowl?	
That's what I like to do.	I3

Ken, whose hands and arms are covered with suds, arrives at the sand table. Jasmine objects.

TEACHER: Let's dry your hands.	I1b
Are you going to be at the water table or the sand?	I1b
KEN: Water table.	
TEACHER: Show me. Where's the water table?	I2
Ken, grinning, points to the balloon table.	
TEACHER (*enjoying the joke with him*): That's the WATER table?	I4a
TEACHER (*to the children at the water table*): What are you going to	
do with all those bubbles? Can you make a beard?	I3
A child tries it.	

Episode: Going on the Train

Several children have built a train of hollow blocks and are taking half a dozen passengers for a ride. Their teacher comes to admire it, asking about the caboose. The children explain.   I3

The teacher observes, "Oh, it's a long train."   I4a

Discussion continues. "Shall I put on the train music?"   I3

She does, and the train starts. Marvin runs to tell the other children, "We going on the choo choo train. Bye! Bye, we're going! See you later, dude!"

The teacher joins the ride.   I2

She and the driver are both given hats. "We going to Chucky Cheese!" says the driver.

The teacher asks, "What are we going to eat when we get there?"   I4a

"Pizza!"

The teacher gets off the train. "We're leaving!" they call.

The teacher requests, "Stop for me on the way back."   I4a

A girl asks the teacher, who is sorting doll clothes in the house area, what she's doing.

"I'm the mom," responds the teacher. "I'm picking up the mess."   I5

Episodes: Telephone Calls

Several children are busy with dolls and phones at a table outdoors.

SOCORRO (*handing a phone to the teacher*): It's your mom.

TEACHER (*into phone*): Hello. How you doing? Did you pick up
that hamburger meat for me? And what else did I tell you to
get? Could you pick up some taco sauce for me—and lettuce
and tomatoes? I'd really appreciate it.   I3

Isabel, who has been skating, takes the phone.

TEACHER: Isabel, I saw you at the roller rink last night. Who were
you skating with? Melissa?   I5

The teacher is soothing Soo-lin, who hurt her leg.   I4b

Lester phones the teacher.

TEACHER: What am I doing?   I4a

LESTER: You're helping Soo-lin.

TEACHER: Yes, I'm helping Soo-lin.   I4a

And I'm having my toast and tea.   I3

Do you know what time it is?   I3

Two children run into the room to look at the clock.

CHILDREN (*running back*): Two minutes! Two minutes, Mrs. Ding!

TEACHER: Thank you. May I have some more hot tea?   I2

Episode: Building a House with Snakes in It

Darrell and Sam have been building with the big blocks. They
find the collection of small animals on the shelf and begin playing
with long wiggly snakes. "Come on, brother, gimme my snake."

DARRELL (*calling to the teacher*): Mrs. Duke, come see our store.

TEACHER: Is it safe for me to come in? Do I have to knock?   I3

BOYS: We got a snake! (*They roar at her.*)

TEACHER: I thought they were nice snakes.   I1b

BOYS: They are. They don't bite.

TEACHER: Okay, then it's safe for me to come in.   I5

BOYS: These are the little snakes. This is the mama.

This is the daddy. They're nice.
TEACHER: Oh, I like nice snakes.   14a

POWER *WITH*, POWER *FOR*, POWER *ON*

At several points in the adult coding scheme, coding definitions are based on the *outcomes* of an adult's behavior rather than on its *intent*. A master teacher isn't only well-meaning. Her interactions with children *work*, accomplishing their intended purposes. They don't work all the time; children are active learners with purposes of their own.

Gretchen: The teacher's "interactions with children work, accomplishing their intended purposes." Whose intended purposes? The children's or the teacher's? Helping children accomplish *their* intended purposes seems more to the point.

Betty: Oh, good question. I'm always getting caught by my own assumptions. My assumption here is, again, value-based; I'm assuming that the teacher is (or should be) purposefully responding to the children's purposes. That's how I'm defining master teaching, as spontaneous behavior in support of children's play—which, in our theory, is "real teaching, directly supporting children's cognitive and social learning."

Gretchen: If we acknowledge children's purposes and give them high priority, as developmentally appropriate practice does, we have to think about power relationships. This style of teaching may make some teachers feel they're giving away the power that is rightfully theirs as adults.

Betty: Responsible adults don't give away their power, but they may make conscious choices to share it with children. Even young children are people with good ideas worthy of respect.

In *The Play's the Thing* (Jones & Reynolds, 1992) we discussed teachers' use of power in their interactions with children. Power exerted *on* a child reflects the teacher's purposes, not the child's; the teacher is in charge and wants to have her way: because that's not safe, because it's cleanup time, because Joey doesn't like it when you call him "Stupid," because it's important that you learn what I have to tell you. This is legitimate teacher behavior; adults *are* in charge, and children often need to put aside their own priorities and go along with those of the adult.

Power exerted *for* a child offers the teacher's power in support of the child's purposes; the teacher facilitates what the child is interested in doing. Power shared *with* a child minimizes, for the present, the teacher's power;

she chooses to follow the child's lead and participate as a peer rather than as the big-person-in-charge.

Each of these types of power is defined, for observation purposes, from the *child's point of view*; the power is classified by its effect rather than by its intention. If a well-meaning adult, genuinely wishing to be supportive, notices a child's struggle with a puzzle piece and says, "May I help you with that?" and gets in response, "No, leave me alone!" it's evident that her intended power *for* has been perceived, and rejected, by the child as threatened power *on*. Not only good intentions, but sensitivity and good timing, are required to exercise power *for*.

It may be especially difficult for teachers to take the child's point of view in the face of cultural and other differences that create a limited basis for shared understanding. As we have noted frequently in this book, teachers use power *on* to control or eliminate play that fails to match their judgment of what's right and proper. Although this response is often appropriate, such impositions of adult power become problematic when the child's play style and play scripts are unfamiliar to, and perhaps uncomfortable for, the teacher. Greer (1993) has written poignantly about her experience as an African-American child in a predominantly European-American school where the Black children's "going to church" play at recess was too loud and dramatic to be acceptable to white teachers. Many children have had similar experiences.

Teachers who find themselves repeatedly interfering with the play of children from backgrounds different from their own (even of a different gender; Vivian Paley, 1984, offers a model in her self-examination of her response to "superheroes in the doll corner") are advised to watch more thoughtfully and ask more questions of both themselves and others. What is the name of this activity, from the child's perspective? Why don't I like it? Is it possible that I might be judging too quickly? Teachers, like children, continue to learn by playing with all the possibilities, not just taking refuge in the familiar.

THE POLITICS OF OBSERVATION

Politics is concerned with the uses of power. In offering tools for coding child and teacher behavior, we are actively aware of their potential for being used *on, for,* or *with* those observed. The power-*on* stance can be seen in the use of assessment tools from a deficit perspective. The object of such assessment—child or adult—is to be remediated, trained in the way he should go as defined by the assessor. Such tools have been developed in play research; Smilansky's early work (1968), for example, focused on the effects of sociodramatic play on "disadvantaged" preschool children and used assessment of play to determine the need for "play training."

Power *on* has a legitimate and necessary place in the planning, implementation, and evaluation of teaching and learning. We do not, however, recommend evaluative use of the tools in this book. Rather, they have been conceptualized within a developmental framework recognizing that the acquisition of play skills, like any other skills, takes place on a continuum of learning, on which unskilled players and master players are at different points. "Master player" is a process description, not an end point to be achieved and tested for. Children need to master tools of all sorts, and play is a tool for learning.

As pointed out earlier, children at play are functioning in the zone of proximal development, in Vygotsky's definition (1933/1978); they're stretching themselves. Vygotsky insists that teaching makes an important contribution to the stretching process. Children learn to play, as they learn language, in the company of more skilled models—peers, older children, and caring adults. Such play relationships involve mentoring, not training; they are based in shared curiosity and collaboration.

Although the research that generated the Child Behavior Inventory had a broad goal of identifying quality in child care, it adopted a primary criterion of "goodness of fit"—is this program an appropriate match for this child? (Prescott et al., 1975). This implies the exercise of teacher power *for* and *with* the child, enabling the teacher to accomplish her purposes while responding to the child's interests, temperament, and culture.

Our conceptualization of teacher development reflects a similar view of the exercise of power, emphasizing growing rather than training (Carter, Jones, & Lakin, 1991; Jones, 1984, 1986a, 1986b, 1993a; Jones & Nimmo, 1994). Like growing children, actively growing teachers also are functioning in a zone of proximal development. To master the teaching of young children, teachers also need many opportunities for initiative taking, problem solving, and innovating within the constraints of reality. Teaching is a profession demanding constant application of higher-order thinking skills. Teachers need to be subjects, not objects, in their own learning (Freire, 1970).

The Teacher Behavior Code is not designed to evaluate teachers for success or failure. Its use calls for power *with* and *for* the teacher, providing her with observational data in the service of her self-chosen growth. The code thus serves as a base for guided self-study by experienced teachers, to be used by the teacher herself or, with her consent, as a basis for dialogue. The observer's responsibility is to serve as scribe and storyteller, reflecting the teacher's behavior back to her through different eyes and voice (Jones,

1993a). The coding offers a second layer of meaning, abstract categories likely to provoke insights only after the first layer — the concrete story — has become familiar and comfortable.

STAGES OF TEACHER DEVELOPMENT

Those responsible for "growing" teachers have a series of obligations. The first is to give good advice. A new teacher is (and needs to be) self-conscious, anxious about her own behavior; and so baseline training provides direct information about the constraints on that behavior: Do this, don't do that. Anxiety-based self-consciousness is a necessary component of the survival stage (Katz, 1977), and it needs to be addressed through direct teaching/training, to get the teacher started.

Past survival, good teachers move quickly to consciousness of the children. Consciousness begins with story (Donaldson, 1978; Egan, 1989), embedded in the drama of the moment: He said, she said, and then off they rode to put out the fire, sirens screaming. Teachers need a whole memory bank of such stories (which the role of trainer as storyteller can help them collect), told as concrete anecdotes, before they're likely to get intrigued by the possibility of analyzing children's stories for patterns. It is at this stage of teacher development (moving beyond survival into consolidation, renewal, and maturity [Katz, 1977]) that some teachers may find the Child's Mode of Behavior coding a useful tool for sharpening their consciousness.

Refocusing on consciousness of *teacher* behavior comes still later in the sequence of growing awareness. The Teacher Behavior Code cannot be used by people unpracticed in observing children's play, because its definitions are dependent on the *child's* purposes and meaning.

We see the Teacher Behavior Code as a tool for use with competent teachers interested in reflecting on their skills in supporting children's play. Analysis of this sort can lead to behaviors that are increasingly both intentional and integrative (made to sustain children's play so that they learn through it, and responsive to the circumstances of the children's play). In the shared process, teachers and children together experience both the spontaneous joy of play and the hard work of learning together.

Laurie Read was the teacher of a wide-age child care classroom at the time of the 1989 earthquake in the San Francisco Bay Area. Earthquakes, like other disasters, are symbolically replayed again and again by the people who have experienced them, children and adults alike. Laurie kept a journal of the children's play during this time, in which her role as master teacher is apparent; our final master players story comes from that journal:

October 18

Nick and John (whose dads are fireman and policeman respectively) had been building firehouses and jails that were crashed by a "bad guy." On the day after the quake they constructed a road remarkably similar to the Cypress structure (where the freeway fell) and alternately crashed and rebuilt all morning.

That afternoon Garth got out the stacking pegs. He was stacking them just high enough to be unstable. He would shake them very gently at first, then violently. When I asked him to explain his game, he said he was playing aftershock. The aftershocks "were the little ones, then comes the BIG ONE" at which time the pegs would fly off the board and go all over the place.

We did some experimenting with the size of buildings — 2-peg buildings were less likely to fall, we decided, than 5 or 6-peg buildings — especially during aftershocks. I asked Garth how tall his house was, and said it was 2 stories tall. He decided his house should be safe since it wasn't as tall as 5 pegs.

November 1

Tanya was on the fire engine. I was rocking it back and forth for the amusement of Jerry (age 2). Tanya popped up: "It's earthquake time!" She laughed and shook it harder. I laughingly suggested she drop and cover. She immediately buried her head into the crook of her arm (while still balancing on the top of the fire engine). Then she told me to do the same. We traded "drop and covers" until she had three other children alternately shaking and covering too.

November 3

Garth made a fabulous, complex city with the blocks. Mark and Kenneth were wrangling over space, trying to work together (or separately) on their building. Kenneth wanted to build it high; Mark wanted to build it long. Little Jerry kept wandering over and brushing against the building. As part of long-standing tradition we kept yelling "Earthquake!" every time the building fell.

Pretty soon Mark said he was going to build a bridge. His bridge connected to Kenneth's falling tower. Mark built a structure that had a slope at one part. He mentioned conversationally that the Bay Bridge fell into the water (a misconception he has had since the quake). We chatted a bit about what had happened during the quake. His bridge was coming close to Garth's building (which had been having its own construction problems).

I asked Garth, who lives in Oakland, if he was building his own city. He said it was Oakland. A minute later he said he was building the Bay Bridge into Oakland. We began discussing the geography of the Bridge; Mark and Garth had just realized that the Bridge connects Oakland to the city, and were deciding how to go about making (or finding) San Francisco. Mark was negotiating with Kenneth when Jerry waded through and caused mass devastation. In the ensuing hysteria the bridge connection was forgotten. Disaster had struck again. (Read, 1992, pp. 21–25)

Teaching the Art of Observation

Elizabeth Prescott

After we had designed the Child Behavior Inventory and used it in our day care research, I created and taught a Pacific Oaks College class called "The Art of Observation." I have taught it as a semester class meeting weekly, as an intensive course lasting 1 or 2 weeks, and as a research seminar where we worked as a team trying to answer certain questions. Most of the students were experienced professionals in a graduate program. If I were working with beginning students, I would take each step more slowly, but I believe I would teach observation in basically the same way, with the Inventory as the starting point. In order to master the study of child development, it's important to have a dependable framework that will make it easy to recognize and name most of the behavior variables that combine in an endless variety of ways. An adult who has become proficient at recognizing the range of child behaviors can analyze them as they happen, deciding whether to intervene or simply to enjoy the action.

When students get their first look at the Inventory, their reaction is anxiety: How could I expect them to learn such a complicated approach to observing a child? (One advantage to teaching this class as an intensive course is that students have no time to get cold feet; they simply have to start and keep going.) Once they begin to get a sense of mastery, there is a feeling of accomplishment and pride in professional growth.

My goals for the students are

1. Learn to focus on one child.
2. Learn to identify transitions and activities and how they happened.
3. Learn to give activities their *true name*.
4. Learn to identify specific codes.
5. Learn to observe characteristics of the physical setting associated with the activity.

6. Practice answering questions by using the code.
7. Reach the stage of flow and develop a comfortable personal way of using this observation instrument.

FOCUSING ON ONE CHILD

The first point I emphasize is that this code was designed to focus on one child. I was surprised when I first discovered how hard it is for students to stop themselves from shifting their attention from one child to another. I should have realized that one of the first skills a good teacher must develop is to scan and keep track of what is going on in all parts of the classroom. This code does not build that skill; instead, it requires total focus on one child. I have found it important to spend some time clarifying this point. The pointed focus does not replace the teacher's roving scan; it is a different tool to be added to the professional repertoire.

IDENTIFYING TRANSITIONS AND ACTIVITIES

Next, I try to create some sense of boundaries in the environment, in order to give the observer a way to keep track of context. I begin by asking the students to think of the child's activities as beads being threaded on a string. In this metaphor the beads are activities and the spacers in between are transitions. For example:

Child wanders around room looking at other children and items on shelves.	Transition
Child selects truck, takes it to rug and begins to play, and so forth.	Activity begins
Another child comes over and says, "Let's do puzzles." They leave rug area.	End of Activity

I want observers to learn how to look at the child's day as a series of activities and transitions, because then it becomes possible to look at a number of characteristics associated with these categories.

At this point I often ask students to choose a partner and go observe. Again I remind them to stay focused on one child and to see if they can agree in their identification of transitions and activities. There are usually questions about whether a real activity developed. I explain that in our research we arbitrarily required a play segment to last 4 minutes before we called it an activity; if it didn't, we labeled it as aborted. Our decision was, of course, arbitrary, but there is a difference between a real chunk of play and the snatches that often are seen.

I have found this a good time to discuss the characteristics of an activity and its natural development. I remind the class that an activity has three components: the play materials and their theme, a place where the activity occurs (e.g., sand area, swings, or doll corner), and a social component (solitary play, best friend, group). Usually, when two of the three components change, the activity ends. For example, Mary and Betsy leave the swings and start digging in the sand. Here the social component remains the same, but the place and play materials change. One of the delights in observing is that there are always grey areas or unexpected changes that can lead to lively discussion and argument among the students.

CODING AN ACTIVITY

At this point I usually ask the students to do another observation. Some like to go in pairs, a choice that then permits them to compare their notes. Others claim they can concentrate better if they observe alone. Since my goal is for everyone to get started, either choice is fine. Usually my initial instructions go something like this.

Select a child and do a detailed 10- to 15-minute observation. If possible, catch the child as she begins an activity. Write on lined paper, using one line for each "move." For example:

Mary puts her hand on the swing chain
Holding the chain, she looks over the yard
She backs into the swing
She pushes off vigorously
She begins to pump, extending both legs firmly
She calls to Betsy, "Hey, Betsy"

When students use this format they are forced to pay close attention to the moment-to-moment flow. Also they can go back more easily to look at beginnings, ends, and transitions, and to note the other circumstances related to their occurrence. When they return to class, they have a written record that can be coded. I ask them to use the code summary (see Table A.1) and to code each line. I also tell them not to agonize over lines that are hard to code, but simply note them for later discussion. I often pair students to code together, and they usually find the coding a bit easier than they had imagined. When they are paired, the coding seems to turn into play, with much laughter and aha's of discovery.

Table A.1 Observation Coding Summary

Rejects	Thrusts	Responds	Integrates
R_1 Ignores intrusion	T_1 Simple physical	E_1 Perceptually responsive: Looks, watches, listens	I_1 Problem solving I_{1a} Shows recognition of built-in constraints I_{1b} Copes effectively with social constraints
R_2 Avoids intrusion	T_2 Gives orders	E_2 Shapes behavior directly to input E_{2a} Obeys, cooperates E_{2b} Imitates	I_2 Child attends with concentration
R_3 Active elimination or negation	T_3 Initiating, thrusting T_{3a} Task T_{3b} Affect	E_2 Superficial or automatic response	I_3 Child adds something new
R_4 Aggressive rejection, active aggression, and/or strong emotion	T_4 Aggressive intrusion T_{4a} Playful T_{4b} Hostile	E_4 Receives rejection, frustration, or pain	I_4 Mutuality in social interaction I_{4a} Reciprocity I_{4b} Offers sympathy, help I_{4c} Hostile reciprocity
	T_5 Asks for assistance from others T_{5a} Task T_{5b} Affect	E_5 Receives help or information E_{5a} Task E_{5b} Affect	I_5 Sees pattern or gives structure
Other U Undifferentiated X_c Verbal exchange unheard	T_6 Gives information, opinion T_{6a} Task T_{6b} Affect	E_6 Responds to questions	I_6 Testing, examining, tinkering
T_E Indeterminate	T_7 Unintentional intrusion	E_7 Perceptive, reflective	

Source: Prescott et al., 1975. Used with permission. Complete definitions of these coding categories can be found on pp. 3–9 of Prescott's book, which is available ($7.50) from the Pacific Oaks College Bookstore, 5 Westmoreland Place, Pasadena, CA 91103. Phone: (818) 397-1330

NAMING THE ACTIVITY

I consider the naming of an activity to be one of the most significant aspects of this approach to coding behavior. The *true name* of the activity is the identification of the child's motivation. For example, an observation that casually might be called Sand Play may have a *true name* of Seeing If You Can Get George to Acknowledge You, or Experimenting with How Many Sand Pies Will Fit on the Bottom of an Overturned Bucket, or Making Roads and Tunnels for Your Red Truck, or Trying to Get the Teacher to Stay Near the Sand Pile. Once students understand the concept of *true name*, it becomes a great source of insight and heated argument. Students also begin to see that some of the specific codes give them useful clues; for example, the "looking and watching" code often suggests what the child is trying to accomplish.

ANSWERING QUESTIONS BY USING THE CODE

Students often are surprised that one session of recording and then coding their observations can give them a feeling of success. When they reach this stage of basic confidence, I ask them to formulate a question that they can answer by use of observation. Here again, I let each student choose whether to work alone or with another student or two. Here are some examples of questions that have been asked and answered.

- Is the long-standing, best-friend relationship between Paul and Judy working well for them?
- Is this tightly structured Montessori program a good fit for George?
- Why does Jimmy always seem like the odd man out?
- Should the wild dramatic play started by John every day be restructured or redirected?
- Why are the teachers always complaining about Mary?

Often the teachers in the programs being observed have questions that students choose to take on as a project. Other students spot a child who interests them or an activity that seems worth following. Once students identify a project, this gives a purpose to their observations. At the last class session students present their projects. Invariably they have found useful answers and are surprised that they could have gotten such a solid answer to their question.

ORGANIZING THE OBSERVATION CLASS

Class time tends to organize itself around questions that students bring from their experience in coding. Invariably, there are discussions about the specific codes. Some colleagues have proposed that instead of learning the specific codes, students could begin by noticing whether a move was thrusting, integrating, or something else. In my experience, however, each code has its own meaning and is more easily learned by giving it recognition. The broad categories—thrusting, responding, and so forth—are more abstract; they acquire meaning as the student works with the code.

The hardest part of teaching this class is the amount of work involved in checking each student's observations. However, in doing this the instructor quickly gets a sense of what is understood and what still needs clarification, for an individual or for the group as a whole. I frequently have been aware of creating new insight in discussion of a particular code with an individual student. It takes some thought to decide how much individual checking is possible and to plan how students can help each other.

I think that it is not necessary to know how to use the code before trying it out on students. If you find yourself interested in learning to use it, I would suggest trying it first in an informal setting such as a seminar or a small group where discussion of a child's individual needs is appropriate. Experience with the code does not alter the fact that it always calls one's attention to something new and unexpected. For that reason I see everyone using it as a learner. When the instructor and students all set out to learn together, a real collaboration develops. The experience of the delights in shared learning may be as valuable to the student as the insights provided by mastery of the code.

One last caveat is that there is no hard and fast right way to work with this code. In doing our research we had to be consistent and rigorous. To use the code for individual purposes permits one the freedom to adapt the recording to one's individual style. Also, there are no absolutely correct answers. Some things are so obvious that there will be no argument, but when situations become ambiguous, wonderful arguments emerge. These opposing viewpoints give students free rein to think, while the code seems to provide them with the vocabulary to communicate. Consequently, you may be surprised at the sophistication of the discussion that ensues.

References

Bateson, G. (1955). *Steps to an ecology of mind*. San Francisco: Chandler.

Berk, L. E. (1994). Vygotsky's theory: The importance of make-believe play. *Young Children, 50*(1), 30–39.

Berk, L. E., & Winsler, A. (1995). *Scaffolding children's learning: Vygotsky and early childhood education*. Washington, DC: National Association for the Education of Young Children.

Bredekamp, S. (Ed.). (1987). *Developmentally appropriate practice in early childhood programs serving children from birth through age 8*. Washington, DC: National Association for the Education of Young Children.

Carini, P. F. (1982). *The school lives of seven children*. Grand Forks: University of North Dakota Press.

Carini, P. F. (1986). Building from children's strengths. *Journal of Education, 3*, 13–24.

Carlsson-Paige, N., & Levin, D. (1987). *The war play dilemma: Balancing needs and values in the early childhood classroom*. New York: Teachers College Press.

Carter, M., Jones, E., & Lakin, M. B. (1991). *Ideas for staff development* (Occasional Paper). Pacific Oaks College, Pasadena, CA.

Creaser, B. H. (1987). *An examination of the four-year-old "master dramatist."* Unpublished master's thesis, Pacific Oaks College, Pasadena, CA.

Csikszentmihalyi, M. (1975). *Beyond boredom and anxiety: The experience of play in work and games*. San Francisco: Jossey-Bass.

Cuffaro, H. K. (1995). *Experimenting with the world: John Dewey and the early childhood classroom*. New York: Teachers College Press.

Daniels, B. (1988). The academics of play. In E. Jones (Ed.), *Reading, writing, and talking with four, five, and six year olds* (pp. 75–84). Pasadena, CA: Pacific Oaks College.

Dansky, J. L., & Silverman, I. W. (1973). Effects of play on associative fluency in preschool children. *Developmental Psychology*, 38–43.

Dewey, J. (1966). *Democracy and education*. New York: Free Press. (Original work published 1916)

Donaldson, M. (1978). *Children's minds*. Glasgow: Fontana/Collins.

Duckworth, E. (1996). *"The having of wonderful ideas" and other essays on teaching and learning* (2nd ed.). New York: Teachers College Press.

Dyson, A. H. (1989). *Multiple worlds of child writers: Friends learning to write*. New York: Teachers College Press.

113

Edwards, C., Gandini, L., & Forman, G. (Eds.). (1993). *The hundred languages of children: The Reggio Emilia approach to early childhood education.* Norwood, NJ: Ablex.

Egan, K. (1987). Literacy and the oral foundations of education. *Harvard Educational Review, 57*(4), 445–472.

Egan, K. (1989). *Teaching as storytelling.* Chicago: University of Chicago Press.

El'konin, D. (1966). Symbolics and its functions in the play of children. *Soviet Education, 7,* 35–41.

Erikson, E. (1950). *Childhood and society.* New York: Norton.

Erikson, E. (1980). *Identity and the life cycle.* New York: Norton.

Farver, J. M. (1993). Cultural differences in scaffolding pretend play: A comparison of American and Mexican mother-child and sibling-child pairs. In K. MacDonald (Ed.), *Parent-child play: Descriptions and implications* (pp. 349–366). Albany: State University of New York Press.

Fein, G. G. (1987). Pretend play: Creativity and consciousness. In D. Gorlitz & J. F. Wohlwill (Eds.), *Curiosity, imagination, and play* (pp. 282–304). Hillsdale, NJ: Erlbaum.

Freire, P. (1970). *Pedagogy of the oppressed.* New York: Seabury.

Genishi, C. (Ed.). (1992). *Ways of assessing children and curriculum: Stories of early childhood practice.* New York: Teachers College Press.

Giffin, H. (1984). The coordination of meaning in the creation of a shared make-believe reality. In I. Bretherton (Ed.), *Symbolic play* (pp. 73–100). Orlando, FL: Academic Press.

Goncu, A. (1993). Development of intersubjectivity in the dyadic play of preschoolers. *Early Childhood Research Quarterly, 8*(1), 99–116.

Gonzalez-Mena, J., & Eyer, D. (1989). *Infants, toddlers, and caregivers.* Mountain View, CA: Mayfield Publishing Company.

Greer, C. (1993). *The culture of play* (Occasional Paper). Pacific Oaks College, Pasadena, CA.

Gronlund, G. (1992). Coping with Ninja Turtle play in my kindergarten classroom. *Young Children, 48*(1), 21–25.

Heath, S. B. (1983). *Ways with words: Language, life and work in communities and classrooms.* Cambridge: Cambridge University Press.

Horney, K. (1945). *Our inner conflicts, a constructive theory of neurosis.* New York: Norton.

Howarth, M. (1989). Rediscovering the power of fairy tales: They help children understand their lives. *Young Children, 45*(1), 58–65.

Huizinga, J. (1950). *Homo ludens.* Boston: Beacon Press.

Hutt, C. (1982). Play and exploration in children. In R. E. Herron & B. Sutton-Smith (Eds.), *Child's play* (pp. 231–251). Malabar, FL: Krieger.

Jervis, K. (1996). *Eyes on the child: Three portfolio stories.* New York: Teachers College Press.

Jones, E. (1984). Training individuals: In the classroom and out. In J. T. Greenman & R. E. Fuqua (Eds.), *Making day care better: Training, evaluation, and the process of change* (pp. 185–201). New York: Teachers College Press.

Jones, E. (1986a). Perspectives on teacher education: Some relations between theory and practice. In L. Katz (Ed.), *Current topics in early childhood education* (pp. 123–141). Norwood, NJ: Ablex.

Jones, E. (1986b). *Teaching adults: An active-learning approach*. Washington, DC: National Association for the Education of Young Children.

Jones, E. (Ed.). (1993a). *Growing teachers: Partnerships in staff development*. Washington, DC: National Association for the Education of Young Children.

Jones, E. (1993b). The play's the thing: Styles of playfulness. *Child Care Information Exchange, 89*, 28–31.

Jones, E., & Meade-Roberts, J. (1991). *Assessment through observation: A profile of developmental outcomes* (Occasional Paper). Pacific Oaks College, Pasadena, CA.

Jones, E., & Nimmo, J. (1994). *Emergent curriculum*. Washington, DC: National Association for the Education of Young Children.

Jones, E., & Reynolds, G. (1992). *The play's the thing: Teachers' roles in children's play*. New York: Teachers College Press.

Katz, L. G. (1977). *Talks with teachers*. Washington, DC: National Association for the Education of Young Children.

Katz, L. G. (1993). What can we learn from Reggio Emilia? In C. Edwards, L. Gandini, & G. Forman (Eds.), *The hundred languages of children: The Reggio Emilia approach to early childhood education* (pp. 19–37). Norwood, NJ: Ablex.

Malaguzzi, L. (1993). History, ideas, and basic philosophy. In C. Edwards, L. Gandini, & G. Forman (Eds.), *The hundred languages of children: The Reggio Emilia approach to early childhood education* (pp. 41–89). Norwood, NJ: Ablex.

McNamee, G. D. (1987). The social origins of narrative skills. In M. Hickman (Ed.), *Social and functional approaches to language and thought* (pp. 287–303). New York: Academic Press.

Paley, V. G. (1984). *Boys and girls: Superheroes in the doll corner*. Chicago: University of Chicago Press.

Paley, V. G. (1986). On listening to what the children say. *Harvard Educational Review, 56*(2), 122–131.

Paley, V. G. (1988). *Bad guys don't have birthdays: Fantasy play at four*. Chicago: University of Chicago Press.

Paley, V. G. (1990). *The boy who would be a helicopter: The uses of storytelling in the classroom*. Cambridge, MA: Harvard University Press.

Paley, V. G. (1992). *You can't say you can't play*. Cambridge, MA: Harvard University Press.

Parten, M. B. (1932). Social play among preschool children. *Journal of Abnormal and Social Psychology, 28*, 136–147.

Pepler, D. (1982). Play and divergent thinking. In D. J. Pepler & K. H. Rubin (Eds.), *The play of children: Current theory and research* (pp. 64–78). New York: Karger.

Piaget, J. (1951). *Play, dreams, and imitation in childhood*. New York: Norton. (Original work published 1945)

Prescott, E., Jones, E., Kritchevsky, S., Milich, C., & Haselhoef, E. (1975). *Assess-*

ment of child rearing environments: An ecological approach: Part II. An envi-ronmental inventory. Pasadena, CA: Pacific Oaks College.

Rabiroff, B., & Prescott, E. (1978). *The invisible child: Challenge to teacher atten-tiveness* (Occasional Paper). Pacific Oaks College, Pasadena, CA.

Read, L. (1992). *Different abilities: A continually emerging curriculum* (Occasional Paper). Pacific Oaks College, Pasadena, CA.

Reynolds, G. (1988). When I was little I used to play a lot. . . . In E. Jones (Ed.), *Reading, writing, and talking with four, five, and six year olds* (pp. 85–90). Pasadena, CA: Pacific Oaks College.

Reynolds, G. (1992). *The role of pretend play in the development of master players.* Unpublished doctoral dissertation, Claremont Graduate School, Claremont, CA.

Rivkin, M. S. (1995). *The great outdoors: Restoring children's right to play outside.* Washington, DC: National Association for the Education of Young Children.

Roskos, K. (1990). A taxonomic view of pretend play activity among 4- and 5-year-old children. *Early Childhood Research Quarterly, 5*(4), 495–512.

Schank, R. C., & Abelson, R. (1977). *Scripts, plans, goals and understanding.* Hillsdale, NJ: Erlbaum.

Skelding, S. (1992). *Activities for supporting non-aggressive play* (Occasional Pa-per). Pacific Oaks College, Pasadena, CA.

Smilansky, S. (1968). *The effects of sociodramatic play on disadvantaged preschool children.* New York: Wiley.

Smilansky, S. (1990). Sociodramatic play: Its relevance to behavior and achieve-ment in school. In E. Klugman & S. Smilansky (Eds.), *Children's play and learning: Perspectives and policy implications* (pp. 18–42). New York: Teachers College Press.

Smilansky, S., & Shefatya, L. (1990). *Facilitating play: A medium for promoting cognitive, socio-emotional and academic development in young children.* Gaith-ersburg, MD: Psychosocial and Educational Publications.

Stritzel, K. (1989). *Block building and gender* (Occasional Paper). Pacific Oaks College, Pasadena, CA.

Sutton-Smith, B. (1985). Play research: State of the art. In J. L. Frost & S. Sunderlin (Eds.), *When children play* (pp. 9–16). Wheaton, MA: Association for Child-hood Education International.

Thornley, K. B. (1988). The writing table: The young child as emergent writer/editor. In E. Jones (Ed.), *Reading, writing, and talking with four, five, and six year olds* (pp. 39–55). Pasadena, CA: Pacific Oaks College.

Torgerson, L. (1994). *Starting with stories* (Occasional Paper). Pacific Oaks Col-lege, Pasadena, CA.

Vygotsky, L. S. (1962). *Thought and language.* Cambridge, MA: M.I.T. Press. (Original work published 1934)

Vygotsky, L. S. (1978). *Mind in society: The development of higher mental pro-cesses.* Cambridge, MA: Harvard University Press. (Original work published 1933)

Wassermann, S. (1990). *Serious players in the primary classroom: Empowering children through active learning experiences.* New York: Teachers College Press.

Wassermann, S. (1993). *Getting down to cases: Learning to teach with case studies.* New York: Teachers College Press.

Werner, E. E. (1984). Resilient children. *Young Children, 40*(1), 68–72.

Wien, C. A. (1995). *Developmentally appropriate practice in "real life": Stories of teacher practical knowledge.* New York: Teachers College Press.

Wolf, D., & Gardner, H. (1979). Style and sequence in early symbolic play. In B. Smith & M. Franklin (Eds.), *Symbolic functioning in childhood* (pp. 117–138). Hillsdale, NJ: Erlbaum.

Index

About the Authors

Gretchen Reynolds is a professor in the Early Childhood Education Program at Algonquin College in Ottawa, Ontario, Canada. She is an adjunct faculty member at Pacific Oaks College in Pasadena, California. She earned a Ph.D. in Education from the Claremont Graduate School in Claremont, California, and an M.S. from Bank Street College of Education in New York City. With Elizabeth Jones she is the co-author of *The Play's the Thing: Teachers' Roles in Children's Play* (1992), published by Teachers College Press. Gretchen has authored several articles.

Elizabeth Jones is a member of the faculty in Human Development at Pacific Oaks College and Children's School in Pasadena, California, where she has taught both adults and children. She earned an M.A. in child development at the University of Wisconsin and a Ph.D. in sociology at the University of Southern California. She collaborated on Elizabeth Prescott's studies over a 10-year period on day care as a child-rearing environment. She has been a visiting lecturer at the University of Alaska and in 1986 was DeLissa Fellow at South Australian College of Advanced Education. She is author of numerous articles and books, including *Dimensions of Teaching-Learning Environments* (with Elizabeth Prescott) (1984), *Teaching Adults: An Active-Learning Approach* (1986), *The Play's the Thing: Teachers' Roles in Children's Play* (with Gretchen Reynolds) (1992), *Emergent Curriculum* (with John Nimmo) (1994); and editor of *Reading, Writing and Talking with Four, Five and Six Year Olds* (1988), *Growing Teachers: Partnerships in Staff Development* (1993), and *Transformational Leadership* (1995).